Sometimes I Don't Like Myself

Sometimes I Don't Like Myself

Candace Schap

Pacific Press Publishing Association
Boise, Idaho
Oshawa, Ontario, Canada

Edited by Bonnie Widicker
Designed by Dennis Ferree
Cover by Steve Smallwood
Typeset in 10/12 Century Schoolbook

Library of Congress Cataloging-in-Publication Data:
Schap, Candace.
    Sometimes I don't like myself: repairing a damaged self-
image / Candace Schap.
        p.   cm.
    Includes bibliographical references.
    ISBN 0-8163-1078-5
    1. Women—United States—Psychology. 2. Self-respect in
women—United States. 3. Self-perception—United States.
I. Title.
HQ1206.S325   1992
155.6'33—dc 20   91-33271
                                                       CIP

92 93 94 95 96 • 5 4 3 2 1

Contents

Dedication

For Melody,
because she overcame

Preface

Self-esteem is the psychological topic of the nineties, especially for women.—Claire Berman.

As we started setting up our lines with bait, I was glad I had let Penny talk me into this fishing trip. I had balked at first, but she had persevered, and here I was.

I hadn't been socially active the previous months. My divorce was still a fresh wound on my heart, and I just didn't feel like doing much. Penny and her husband couldn't stand to see me moping. They had tried fixing me up on dates or inviting me to go places where I could meet men, but I wasn't ready.

A fishing trip sounded safe though. Another married couple I had never met were going along, so the day would be spent in a nonthreatening atmosphere.

Randy and Pat proved to be an interesting couple, holdovers from the hippie era. She wore an ankle-length flowered skirt, and her hair hung long and straight down her back. He, too, had long hair, and his face was obscured with a bushy beard and mustache. The only thing belying his attempt to look youthful was the paunch hanging over his tightly belted jeans. I liked this casual, laid-back pair right away.

We fished a little, picnicked a little, and laughed and talked a lot. I felt more relaxed than I had in a long time as I enjoyed the company of the two friendly, outgoing couples.

Afternoon came, and the sun grew hot. Pat finally announced, "I'm going to the van to take a nap. It's too hot out here for me."

When she was gone, Randy came to sit beside me. As always, I felt awkward trying to make conversation. In most situations I was wary of saying the wrong thing and making a fool of myself. I was afraid to be me, afraid people wouldn't like that person.

But Randy was friendly and seemed to really enjoy conversing with me. I was elated by this much-needed acceptance after the cruel rejection of my divorce.

Soon Penny's husband, Don, noted that we were low on bait. "Let me go for more," I said, jumping to my feet. "I'd enjoy the walk to the bait shop."

Standing beside me, Randy said casually, "I'll go with you. A walk sounds nice."

So together we crossed the sandy beach toward the road. We were not even out of sight of his van when Randy nonchalantly moved closer to me and slipped an arm around my waist.

I froze. As we walked, my mind raced in an attempt to understand. In clear view of his wife, he was making a pass at me. Only moments before, his acceptance had been exhilarating. Now I panicked, not knowing what to do.

I wanted to remove his hand from my waist, but I was afraid. Though I couldn't have verbalized my thoughts at the time, what was running through my mind went something like this: If I remove his hand, he'll get angry or embarrassed. I can't do that to him. If I do, he won't like me anymore.

I was flushed, my face burning with shame and fear. My stomach felt as though it had dropped through a bottomless pit. I tried to evaluate my dilemma. If I didn't move his hand, he'd think I was encouraging him. If I did, he'd be angry at me. Which outcome would be worse?

Then as clear as if it had been spoken aloud to me, the thought came, What's wrong with you, anyway? He's the one who's wrong, not you! He's the one with a wife sleeping trustingly in the van. You cannot worry about his feelings!

Without a word I reached down and removed his hand.

"You're one of those," he snarled softy, as he turned and walked away. He didn't speak to me again, that day or ever.

What a moment of truth that was for me, having so graphically demonstrated just how low my insecurities had taken me. A married man had made a pass at me, and I had worried about hurting his feelings. I had nearly gone along with him rather than run the risk of losing his approval!

Low self-esteem, insecurities, nonassertive personality— whatever you call it, the effect is the same. Fear of rejection, of not gaining others' acceptance or approval, is paralyzing. You become a people pleaser, not because you like to see others happy, but because you hope it will make them like you.

Low self-esteem caused me to date men I didn't like or who were completely wrong for me, to volunteer for jobs I neither wanted nor was particularly qualified to perform, and to compromise my values in the hope of receiving a little approval from people I quite often didn't like that much anyway.

That day on the beach I realized just how far I'd gone in my desperate search for love and acceptance. From childhood into my teen years and then into a bad marriage, I had made choices largely on what I thought would gain others' approval and not on what I thought would be best for me. How many times had I found myself in similar situations, miserable and ashamed, but without the strength of character or beliefs to do what I knew was right for me? Too many times.

But even as I was berating myself for being a spineless wimp, I realized something else. The experience had a positive side. After all, I *had* stood up for my convictions. Maybe I hadn't been particularly forceful in doing so, but I had finally done what I knew was right, in spite of my fear of rejection. And even more amazing, when he had indeed rejected me, I had survived!

In fact, I had felt a wonderful peace once I removed his

hand from my waist. The consequences had not changed that peace. Gone was the sick stomach, the pounding head, and the trembling hands. Doing the right thing had given me peace! This was an amazing revelation. It was possible to suffer rejection and not be devastated by it. A simple revelation, but life-changing for me. That day I began a journey that would take years to complete but that has had wonderfully satisfying results. The beginning of the journey was to get to know myself, because after all the years of hiding the real me from the world, even I didn't know who I really was.

I began a journey through self-discovery toward self-acceptance. It took me into a deeper, profoundly loving relationship with God. It took me into situations and relationships I would never have thought myself capable of handling. In the end, I learned how to like myself, even when I don't like myself.

Introduction

While we have done such marvelous things in science and manufacturing and the conquest of space, we have left the spirit of man the greatest undeveloped, unexplored area in all of life. The dark country of earth is the soul of man. How few people are really, thrillingly, tinglingly alive right down to their fingertips.—**T. Cecil Myers.**

"I'm convinced that almost everyone suffers from a lack of self-esteem in some form at some time."

That statement was made at my church's weekly Bible study to a group of about fifteen women. Very different women. Look at any group of women or men* and you'll find fascinating variety. The quiet, reserved one; the self-starter, always involved in a new project; the wise-sounding older one; the bubbly one; the sophisticated one; the class clown.

No matter what part of the group, nearly all will nod their heads in a moment of identification with the statement that everyone feels low self-esteem.

Insecurities abound. Some are openly timid and shy; others, like myself, manage to mask our self-doubts. Most people see me as outgoing and self-assured. They would be

*In a study done by the Minnesota Department of Education, it was discovered that in sixth grade, both male and female students had healthy self-images. By the ninth grade, however, girls were twice as likely as boys to have self-esteem problems. To learn more about the reasons for this disparity, you can read "How to Make Yourself a Stronger Person" by Claire Berman (*Ladies' Home Journal*, November 1990).

surprised to see the anxiety I suffer sometimes in doing something so simple as initiating a conversation.

What makes us so down on ourselves so much of the time? And better yet, what can we do to change it?

If you are looking for knowledge from a trained therapist or psychiatrist, this is not the book for you. I have read many books by these people, some extremely helpful, some not. This is not one of those books. However, I do consider myself an expert in understanding low self-esteem. That's why I'm writing—to let you know you're not the only one fighting the battle for healthy self-esteem. I want you to know that it is possible for you to change your life for the better.

Everyone can't approach the problem in the same way. The Type-A personality and the shy violet obviously have to find ways that suit their particular personality types. But some basic principles apply to all personalities and are useful to anyone struggling for self-acceptance. A variety of factors may have caused the problem, but the solution has steps common for all.

We've all heard the horror stories. Many emotional disorders such as obesity or bulimia, sexual promiscuity, and alcoholism have their roots in low self-esteem. But those are the extremes. If you can't identify with these tragic practices, you might recognize yourself in another category.

Mary Ann L. Diorio, Ph.D., lists twenty symptoms of low self-esteem. Do you find yourself on this list anywhere? I think you will agree that these symptoms are much more common than those in the previous paragraph.

1. A sense of unworthiness
2. Difficulty relating to people
3. Perfectionism
4. Inappropriate emotional responses
5. Fear
6. Touchiness and irritability
7. An inordinate concern about others' opinions
8. A critical spirit
9. Dependence on others

10. Difficulty accepting compliments
11. Worry
12. An overly scrupulous conscience
13. A legalistic attitude toward God and religion
14. Use of anger as a defense mechanism
15. A lack of transparency
16. Workaholism
17. Difficulty expressing emotions
18. Finding security in material possessions
19. An attitude of passivity
20. A sense of being inferior or superior to others

("The Secret Life of Parents," *Christian Parenting Today*, March/April 1991, p. 56.)

In his book *His Image . . . My Image*, Josh McDowell has his own list of thirty-two results of a poor self-image, including "a habit of letting others 'walk' on them," "fear of being alone," "a sense of masculinity or femininity felt only through sexual conquests," and "a striving to become something or somebody instead of relaxing and enjoying who they are."

Why struggle to change? Our self-image is directly related to the way we make decisions that will affect the rest of our lives—from whom we marry to what job we'll take to how we discipline our children. Fear of rejection or fear of losing someone's approval can cause us to make many unwise choices.

But beyond the way our insecurities affect our own lives is the effect on those around us. A friend of mine who is in charge of Christian education at her church was recently bemoaning the scarcity of people willing to take leadership roles. "Lots of people out there would make great teachers, or have something really worthwhile to contribute," she said in frustration. "The problem comes in making them believe it."

If you see yourself in that sentence, you're not alone. There are things to be done, and the workers aren't coming forward. I don't believe that laziness or complacency can entirely explain the problem. I think a large number of competent, willing people are just plain afraid. Afraid that if they try, they'll fail, and people will think less of them.

For the Christian, the journey toward healthy self-esteem starts with God. Every journey has to if we hope to discover the best within ourselves. Non-Christians can make the journey and, through counseling or therapy, attain a level of healing. But they will never experience the most wonderful gift of all—the unconditional love and forgiveness of God.

If you are looking for a get-well-quick, ten-days-to-a-new-you sort of solution, you will not find it here. Any journey that we begin with Christ will take time. He knows our hearts, but it usually takes a lot of heel dragging and denial on our part before we listen to what He's telling us.

My journey has taken years and indeed is ongoing. I hope that my experience and that of other women will help to make your trip a little easier or will help you to get through a painful step a little quicker, but don't plan on being changed overnight. God wants to change you right, from the inside out. He wants to take time on the little things that may seem unimportant to you but that He knows will keep you from your goal if they are not tended to at the outset.

As you begin reading, then, determine that you will start the journey with Him. Look to your heart first, then to the practical side of change. If you reverse the order, you will probably find yourself starting all over again somewhere down the road.

My hope is that this book will help you out of your protective shell and into the light. Talents, leadership ability, evangelistic ministry, friendship—all these things lie wasting in the dead sea called Fear of Rejection. We can cross this sea with the God who parts the waters and come out on the other side triumphant, productive people.

Chapter 1

The Not-Good-Enoughs

Don't pay any attention to me. Nobody ever does.—**Eyeore.**

A VW "Bug" was the "in" car. Anyone who was "cool" either wanted one or had one. The young couple sitting in the front seat had one. And I was lucky enough, along with my best friend, to be sitting in the back seat.

I was thirteen years old. Thirteen is a pretty traumatic age to be no matter who you are. Everyone is either plump and awkward or skinny and awkward. I was the latter. (When I got older in a household with two well-endowed sisters, one would jokingly call me the runt of the litter. Luckily she didn't say it when I was thirteen, or it would have shattered me.)

We were zipping down the highway on the way from Florida to Georgia. It was my first year to go away for a week of Bible camp for teenagers, and I was excited. Tom and Patty Green were going as counselors.

They were in their twenties and so freshly married that they seemed like teenagers themselves. They laughed and talked with Janice and me, and I fell in love with them. Could they really be that interested in what I had to say? In my interests, in my dreams? They seemed to be. They kept asking us questions and making us feel as though the answers were important to them.

And they laughed at my jokes. I was discovering that if I could make someone laugh, I felt accepted. And this wonderful young couple kept laughing at the things I said,

17

making me feel very accepted.

It was only natural that when we arrived at the campground, Janice and I would try to nurture this new-found relationship. We sought them out in the mess hall; we tried to sit with them in chapel. During our free time we would hike to the top of the hill where the wild blackberries grew because Tom had expressed a real fondness for them. While we were at it, we filled cups with wildflowers for their room.

A few days later, our church group made plans to meet in the parking lot so that we could drive to one of the local attractions. Janice and I happily ran over to the Greens' little VW, only to be brought up short by a horrifying sight. They already had some of the older teens in the back seat. Our back seat.

I wish I could say the rest of the day was a blur in my memory. It isn't. I remember all too well the tears that filled my eyes as Patty smiled brightly and said, "Sorry, kids, but someone else is riding with us today!" Those tears worked their way into a full-blown sobbing pity party as we found another vehicle, and they didn't stop until I was threatened by my older sister.

I acted like a jerk. That memory is embarrassing to me, but what's even worse, I can still feel the terrible hurt that made me want everyone to know it was time to pay attention. You see, Tom and Patty had done more than just give my seat away and hurt my feelings. Tom and Patty had given proof to the one great fear that lived within my still-young heart—if people got to know the real me, they wouldn't like me anymore.

Why I felt that way I still don't know. Unlike some who can point to domineering, abusive, or neglectful parents, mine were pretty nice people. Sure, they had their faults and their own problems, but they never put me down or talked as though I were inferior.

I suspect that being a middle child had a lot to do with it. My older sister was always so smart, so mature. She had a tightknit group of friends, and they all seemed to love her.

When she became a Christian, she was so much more spiritual than I could ever be. She did everything right, and in my own eyes I could never measure up. My younger sister was cute and funny. She was the baby everyone loved and laughed at.

No one ever told me I wasn't as cute, funny, or smart as the other two. I just felt it. I couldn't find a niche for myself, and so I thought there wasn't one. I'm sure once I was in that emotional condition, other events that occurred as I grew up only helped to reinforce my insecurity.

In the sixth grade, when one of my best friends yelled at me for being mean to her little sister, I slapped her across the face. I was as horrified as she that I had done it. And even at that young age, I knew I had done it because I couldn't stand to hear her being angry with me. I just wanted to make her words stop; I didn't mean to hurt her.

From that early age with my girlfriends, and then on into my dating years with young men, I never felt secure in a relationship. I was always waiting for them to "find me out," to discover that I wasn't the person they thought but really someone quite unlikable.

That's not a very pleasant way to spend your life. If I had been able to look at the facts, I would have known it wasn't true. I never lacked for a best friend, and she was always an attractive person. My two boyfriends in high school were both very good-looking, and the relationships lasted for months.

But I wasn't able to take a rational look at the facts. I only knew what my fearful heart was telling me. While the other girls were filling out and getting a figure, I stayed skinny. Like all young girls, I was certain if someone would just get past my physical appearance and get to know me, they would love me. But once they got past the physical appearance, then the fear gripped me that it wouldn't last for long. Sooner or later they'd discover they had been taken in.

I didn't know then, of course, that the term for my condition was low self-esteem. I didn't know anything about technical language or what the pop psychology of the day was. Even today I like to keep away from trendy terminology. I keep it plain and simple. What I call my condition, or my disease, is the "not-good-enoughs." That strips it of all the fancy jargon and calls it what it is. I had a strong case of the not-good-enoughs, and it was making a cripple out of me.

When I entered high school, I had a plan. It was going to help me break out of my shell and get me the approval I needed to become "good enough." In high school, the separation between the "classes" becomes much more defined. There you receive your "ranking," and there is no breaking out of it. We had the "in" group, which in those days were the Surfers. There were the Greasers on the other end of the spectrum and of course a group for the brainy kids who were not good at socializing. I fell somewhere in between, but like every other "out" person, I longed to be "in."

There was a uniform that went along with being "in." The brand name of the day was Villager, and that was what all the girls who were well liked wore. It consisted of button-down tailored shirts, A-line skirts with the brand-new feature of a zipper in the front, and penny loafers.

My plan centered around that uniform. I worked at my summer job until I had saved enough to buy it. On the first day of school, I walked proudly down the hall, watching out of the corner of my eye for the looks of appreciation, the nods of acceptance. They never came. No one noticed. No one noticed that this year I was "in." No one cared.

Nothing had changed. Though I had a close circle of friends, I felt rejected because none of the "in" crowd wanted me. It was about that time that I learned the value of being outrageous, just a little bit different. If I wasn't trying to be accepted by them, I couldn't be rejected.

In Florida in the late sixties, surfing was the "in" thing. Even though the Beatles were popular, the Carnaby Street look had not yet caught on. We were into Villager, bikinis, jams, and dark, dark tans. But when the uniform didn't work, I turned to the mod look of the Beatles, even to having my hair cut in their trademark pudding bowl. I wore wildly flowered bell-bottoms with matching vests that I made myself from upholstery fabric. When I wore dresses, I completed the ensemble with white fishnet stockings. To the outside world I looked like a self-confident girl who had developed her own look. Inside, I loved the look because it separated me from those who had rejected me. It protected me from the hurt of trying to conform and not succeeding. Now I couldn't be a part of the "in" crowd no matter what. By being outrageous, by setting myself apart, I had eliminated the chance of rejection because I could pretend I didn't want in anyway.

The not-good-enoughs hurt me academically as well. As a sophomore, I made top grades in classes like biology and geometry, subjects others were struggling with. This was a wonderful discovery for me, because for the first time I excelled in something. I was better than someone else. I remember lying in bed with my younger sister one night, telling her my plans to graduate summa cum laude and then go on to medical school.

But the not-good-enoughs ate away at me. The little voice inside kept telling me I could never make it, and I began to believe the little voice. When I was a junior, I took chemistry. Before then, I had breezed through every bit of math and science I had taken. Suddenly, I met a formidable opponent. Chemistry class might as well have been taught in a foreign language. I simply could not get it, no matter how much after-school help I got, no matter how long I puzzled over a word problem. In the end my teacher gave me a C, only because he knew I had tried so hard.

Now, besides feeling I was a social failure, I had also discovered I wasn't so smart either. Just one more area where I was afraid people might discover the true me. But the not-good-enoughs had a grip on me, so instead of working harder or simply changing my career aspirations, I gave up.

Chemistry is the only course I ever got a C in, yet I took that as proof that I couldn't make it. I found with a minimum of effort I could easily produce B's and some A's, so I settled for that. After all, if I didn't shoot too high, I couldn't fall short, right? Besides, I really didn't feel like getting any further proof that I was a loser. If I settled for second best, first best couldn't reject me.

If I didn't set myself a lofty goal, I couldn't fail. As I had done with the uniform, I pulled myself out of the game. Temporarily, I put a stop to the little voices that told me I couldn't measure up. I wasn't even trying, so what was the difference?

When I was a junior, I dated a good-looking college student. When a senior, I found true love with a darling young motorcycle rider who seemed to adore me. Neither of these relationships was enough to convince me that I was lovable. I went with the young man in my senior year for nine months. During that entire time, I doubt that we ever had a truly meaningful conversation, mainly because I never felt secure enough just to be myself with him. I was always awkward on dates, afraid I would somehow make a fool of myself. All my friends assumed we would someday get married, but the thought panicked me. How on earth could I marry someone with whom I couldn't even have a conversation?

Where did God fit into all this? I think the saddest result of my not-good-enoughs came in my relationship with Him. Instead of becoming the new creation that Scripture talks about, I still wallowed in a mire of self-pity and self-hate. I knew the Lord, or thought I did, but it wasn't making a difference.

When I was twelve years old, my mother started taking us to a new church. There she found a new understanding of God, and one night as she tucked us into bed, she told us what had happened.

"Remember how we used to think that if you tried really hard to be good, you might someday make it into heaven?" I lay at the end of my bunkbed and nodded. "Well, I've found out it isn't like that at all."

This was interesting news to me, as you can well imagine. I had always wondered how someone with the not-good-enoughs was ever going to make it into heaven. So I was all ears.

"I've learned at our new church that because you can never be good enough to go to heaven, Jesus died on the cross for your sins. All you have to do is believe and accept Jesus' gift to you." While I could see she was very happy with this news, it confused me a bit. I had always believed that Jesus died on the cross for my sins. That's who Jesus was—the man who died on the cross to save the world. I just had never understood what to do with that information.

That summer at Bible camp, I learned. There I heard the entire story of Jesus' life, death, and resurrection. I couldn't hear enough as it all started making sense. God did love me. He did care about what happened to me, and He had made a way for me to be good enough to get to heaven.

I lay on my cot that night, watching the moon through the window and talking to God for hours. I made everything right with Him as I confessed my sins and gave my heart to Him.

I was excited about starting my new life as a Christian. Because I really didn't know much about being a Christian, I was vulnerable to whatever teaching came my way. Unfortunately, we moved again, and the church I began attending only confused me further.

Not that the people in that congregation weren't good Christian people. But they talked so much about following the rules that I totally missed the part about having a personal relationship with Jesus. As they saw it, if you followed the rules, you were a good Christian, and God would smile on you. If you didn't follow the rules, you were considered "backslidden," and God would not be pleased. At that point you would have to go forward in church and "rededicate" your life. Once again the burden of being "good enough" had fallen back on me and my own human strength and efforts.

I'm not saying rules are necessarily bad. Rules can be

bad, though, when you try to make them do what they aren't intended to do. Unfortunately, I knew nothing about living by faith, about the indwelling Christ who would help me live a life pleasing to Him. All I knew were the rules I was being given.

They told me not to go dancing, they told me not to go to movies, they told me not to play cards, they told me not to wear slacks. Bowling was bad because there was liquor served on the premises, and skating was bad because of the distinct possibility of bodily contact with the opposite sex. The list went on and on. Instead of enjoying my newfound relationship with God, I was having a terrible time trying to keep up with what I could and couldn't do.

None of those rules were bad in themselves. Indeed, many people have made the choice of conscience to abstain from these activities. When done because you feel it enhances your Christian witness, it can be a beautiful testimony. When done because you're afraid God won't like you otherwise, it turns your testimony sour.

Because of the unbalanced teaching I received, I ended up with a warped idea of the nature of God. I understood Jesus as a form of glorified fire insurance—He had saved me from the fires of hell, but that was as far as His involvement went. And God was the Great Guilty Conscience in the Sky. You know, "He sees you when you're sleeping, He knows when you're awake; He knows if you've been bad or good, so be good for goodness' sake!"

Soon I found I couldn't keep all the rules. Many of them were against things that I, as a teenager, liked to do with my friends. So I did them anyway and then lived with the guilt that, even in God's eyes, I just couldn't be good enough. Perhaps good enough to be saved but not good enough to be a witness for Him or live a life pleasing to Him.

My solution to this dilemma was the same one I'd used in school when I tried to wear the uniform of the "in" crowd or had tried to be a star student. If I wasn't good enough, I would just give up. If I wasn't trying to live up to the high standards called for in the rules, I couldn't be a failure, right?

By the time I graduated from high school, I was pretty messed up inside. I had failed at everything that had been important to me. My personal relationships were often in turmoil because I was constantly trying to be whatever I thought others wanted me to be. I had lots of dreams but no confidence in myself to go after them. And God had been pushed to one side in my life.

And that was only adolescence. I had no idea that adult not-good-enoughs were about to strike, and strike hard.

Chapter 2

Knowing the Enemy

The childhood feelings we remember are fully alive today and remind us that the world around us was, and assumedly still is, stronger than we are.—**Josh McDowell.**

When I play chess, I have absolutely no strategy. I move my pieces whenever it looks like I need to run from someone. When I see the possibility of capturing my opponent's piece, I don't look ahead to see if he has laid a trap for me, giving me a lesser piece in order to put my King in check. I don't plan, I don't plot, I don't try to understand my opponent's thinking. That's why I hate chess, because invariably, my opponent is planning, plotting, and studying me. And invariably my opponent wins.

Many of us move through life a lot like the way I play chess. We have no idea danger is around us until suddenly we are blindsided. Then we stagger around, concentrating on getting our equilibrium back, wanting only to get things patched up so we can plunge blindly forward again.

Whether it's winning at chess or winning at life, strategy is crucial. And to have a strategy, we have to know and understand the opponent. When a football team is preparing for a game, they watch game films of the opposing team, studying their moves in depth. Then each player studies the individual he will be playing against, finding his weaknesses and strengths so he can be prepared to take advantage of them or defend against them.

We need to take the battles going on in our daily lives

just as seriously. Instead of plunging ahead, making mistake after mistake, throwing on temporary patches, and wondering why we don't have control, we need to take the time to identify and study our enemies.

Sometimes the victim of low self-esteem is like the alcoholic. She needs to stand up and say, "Hello, I'm Jane Doe, and I don't like myself." A simple statement, but for the first time, the problem has been brought down into simple, understandable terms. If I can identify the problem, I will then be able to look for causes and cures.

For many people, discovering why they are so insecure, why they have so little healthy love for self, is an important first step in the process of healing.

Sometimes the help of a therapist who knows how to dig for the answers will be necessary. If you have been abused or have had a deeply traumatic experience in your life, perhaps you will need someone with expertise to help you work through it. Severe depression needs to be dealt with immediately by a professional, sometimes even with medication.

My friend Tina and her husband are excellent examples of people who need professional help. Both of them suffer from poor self-esteem. Tina is simply reluctant to put herself forward, to be assertive or outgoing. Her husband's situation has been far different.

After a series of setbacks, he became so convinced of his total worthlessness that he slid into deep depression. After a couple of years, he began thinking of suicide. At that point, he sought help. Now receiving counseling and medication, he is improving every day. But the basis of his trauma is that he just didn't like himself and felt he deserved all the bad things that were happening to him.

I mention this couple because, while I firmly believe we can do many things to help ourselves, we need to be careful when the problems run too deep. It is dangerous to play armchair psychiatrist when the situation calls for someone trained in handling the deep traumas of the human psyche.

However, I don't think professional help is always called

for in discovering the reasons and the cures for a poor self-image. We have to be willing to work and to face ourselves honestly, but it can be done.

Sometimes self-evaluation looks too daunting. When I stood back and looked at it, my life appeared to be just one big mess. I didn't know where to start work, much less what it was I was working toward. In fact, at that point in my life, I wasn't even thinking about working on anything because I didn't know anything could be done to change the mess of my life.

Once I did begin to work on change, I was amazed to discover how much could be traced back to my childhood and teen years.

In my youth, I doubt I could have told you what was good about myself. Even when I thought I had discovered something, I soon would do something to make me think I had been deceiving myself. But now, as an adult, one of the most crucial things I need to do for my self-esteem is to know my strengths, the armor I can take into battle with me.

To inventory the armor available to you, start by making a list of your strong points, the things about you that are "good enough." If you've lived a long time belittling yourself and your abilities, this might be a difficult assignment. In his book *His Image . . . My Image*, Josh McDowell asks the reader to make two lists. One should contain five of the person's strong points, the other, five of his or her weaknesses. Then McDowell asks a telling question: Which list of characteristics took longer to identify?

Sometimes you may have to go to someone else and ask, "What do you see good in me? Is there anything about me that you particularly like? Is there any positive way in which I touch people's lives?" If you can be objective, ask yourself those questions, but answer honestly!

Once you have found your strong points, nurture them. These are the tools you will draw on to fight the not-good-enoughs once the battle has begun.

Once you've taken care of arming yourself, the next step

is to study your opponent so you'll know how to fight it. You need to have your enemy clearly defined. This is more than latching on to some generic catch-all term. To say "I'm shy" tells you nothing. Shyness is not your enemy. It is a symptom of the not-good-enoughs, not a reason for them. Anger, hostility, complacency, depression, extreme submissiveness—all these are symptoms, not reasons.

What are reasons? One place reasons are commonly found is in your relationship with one or both parents. Did you feel rejected by your mother or your father at some point in your life? Was there a divorce or a death? Perhaps you had a parent who openly showed preference for one of your siblings. Perhaps you had a parent who never praised your good work but always took note of your mistakes. Maybe both parents had to work, and you interpreted it that they were trying to avoid being with you. As you can see, the possibilities are endless. Only after having children myself did I realize the myriad ways I could injure their self-esteem without even knowing I was doing it.

An important thing to note as you sort through your childhood is that a lot of problems stem from your perception, not necessarily from deliberate acts of others. For example, consider a father who dotes on his babies but doesn't know how to communicate with an adolescent. He pulls back as the child matures, unsure of himself. What the child sees is a dad who used to lavish time and affection on him but now doesn't seem to care. The child perceives rejection where none was intended. Unfortunately, this perception is carried through life.

As you define your enemy and find your reasons, it is not necessary to blame other individuals. Understanding their role in your problems is necessary, but blaming them will only avoid taking the responsibility of accepting who you are. Too many people are limping through life saying, "It's not my fault I'm like this. My mother/father/significant other did this to me."

Another area to examine for reasons could be an illness or a physical impairment. Was there something about you that made you feel different from everyone else? Maybe as an adult you have come to accept that difference, but the old hurts have turned you into a withdrawn person, afraid to take chances. Did an illness keep you out of the social whirl during some crucial years, so that now you feel you have nothing to offer in social relationships?

Was there a traumatic event in your history? The death of a parent or a sibling can cause self-hatred. Even those who aren't born with the not-good-enoughs can contract them from an incident that causes self-loathing and condemnation. Many children carry the scars of molestation with them into their adult lives, blaming themselves and feeling unworthy as human beings.

Even when we have named our enemies, it may be difficult to understand the way we have responded to these life challenges. My friend June is in her seventies now, but when she was a child, she was constantly beaten. Today you would never know it. June always takes the positive outlook on things, and even when something upsets her, she doesn't let it consume her. She is the one we all go to when we need a calming word of wisdom to help us on our way. When people talk about not liking themselves, she doesn't relate at all.

I look at June and then at myself. I had a relatively happy childhood with parents and family who loved and cared for me. Why did June turn out to be the person we all want to be, and I end up feeling like a social misfit?

Obviously, just knowing the reasons for your poor self-image isn't all there is to it. While the outward factors of environment, parental temperament, and physical well-being certainly start you out with certain perceptions of life, those perceptions can be modified, exaggerated, or in some other way changed by inward factors. Inward factors are those personality elements that make you *you*.

1. *Birth order*

"I'm either going to have two children or four children," I heard a young woman saying.

"Why is that?" I asked her.

"Because," she said earnestly, "I'll never let some poor child of mine end up being the middle child."

I used to think it a myth that birth order could be an accurate predictor of how a person would respond to life. Now I know better—the middle-child syndrome really exists. In fact, it's not limited to the middle child. Certain patterns are followed by a majority of people, depending on where they were born in their family structure. This is one of the inward factors. The outward factors will work together with it to make your personality different from some other firstborn down the block, but by and large, the trends are the same.

I wish I had known such things when I was growing up. It would have helped me enormously to have been able to say, "I'm not different from everyone else in the world. This is all a normal response given my birth order, my personality type, etc." Of course, one of the unfortunate realities of being a teenager is believing that you are different, and all the wisdom in the world doesn't change that thinking. It would have helped me as I faced adulthood though, had I understood my weaknesses as part of a normal process instead of something that made me unacceptable.

Dr. Kevin Leman, in his *Birth Order Book*, says, "Whenever I mention 'birth order' during a seminar or a counseling session, I'm often met with the same question: 'Birth order—is that like astrology?' " His reply is that birth order "has nothing to do with astrology, but it definitely affects your personality, whom you marry, your children, your occupational choice, and even how well you get along with God" (p. 10).

When I read Dr. Leman's book, I found an accurate description of myself and my insecurities. How did he know me so well? Because he was describing the classic example of a middle child, which is what I am.

I want to stress that neither birth order nor temperament type, which I will discuss next, can give anyone his or her complete psychological picture. They are merely tools for helping us understand ourselves and getting us started on the road to change. They come at the beginning of the process; they are not the cure-all. As I said earlier, real, lasting change doesn't come quickly. It takes long, hard work.

But there is a real, positive aspect to the whole area of birth order. As Dr. Leman says, "As important as a child's order of birth may be, it is only an influence, not a final fact of life forever set in cement and unchangeable as far as how that child will turn out" (p. 182).

Although nothing could change where I had been born into my family, it was helpful for me to recognize that much of the pain of rejection I felt was caused by my inability to find where I fit in and also that much of it was self-induced pain. My parents had not loved me any more or any less than my other siblings. Once I sorted through all the slights and pains I had suffered, real or imagined, and recognized them for what they were, they no longer could control me. Now, when old hurts try to come up disguised as new hurts, I know their voices, and I tell them No.

Middle-child syndrome is only one aspect of birth-order psychology one needs to understand. Certainly firstborn children come with all sorts of built-in pressures and expectations imposed on them. I asked a friend of mine what number she was in her family, thinking I could do a quick personality rundown on her. When she answered that she had been the first, I was surprised. She didn't fit the firstborn image of overachiever and perfectionist. When I told her this, she smiled knowingly.

"You forget there are two kinds of firstborns," she said. "Many feel they have to be perfect and work at it all their lives. Others feel they're supposed to be perfect but know they aren't and never will be. They just give up trying and then spend the rest of their lives pretending they don't care. That's me."

It's no easy road for the baby of the family, either, as can be seen in the experience of my younger sister. Melody is two years younger than I and is the sister who got all the attention as the cute, funny baby of the family. However, when Melody was seven, my mother brought home a new baby and, over the next few years, added two more. Melody was completely dethroned as The Baby.

Whereas I had never really found where I fit into the family structure, Melody thought she had found her niche and had been doing quite well in it. Without warning, she was shoved out of her niche and was devastated by the rejection she felt. She rapidly put on weight, became the "rebel" of the family, had a disastrous first marriage, and struggled with low self-esteem. It wasn't until she was secure in her relationship and value to God that she was able to deal with the weight problem and make a strong marriage.

During our adult years, I didn't see much of Melody. We lived across the country from each other and had large families to care for. But from my viewpoint, she looked like someone who had named her enemies and triumphed over them. I found out only recently that the not-good-enoughs had continued to plague her all her life.

In October 1990, Melody was struck with a sudden brain hemorrhage, and three days later she died at the age of thirty-nine. At her wake, I was overwhelmed with the number of friends who came to tell me how Melody had positively affected their lives. She had a very giving nature, and one and all knew they could count on her to drop everything to lend a hand if they needed it. I was wonderfully surprised to learn what a beautiful and fulfilled woman my sister had become.

When the wake ended, several family members went over to the coffin to say our final goodbyes. Her husband's softly spoken words stunned me. "Oh, Melody," he said, "you would have loved this. You never thought that people really liked you."

Yet she had overcome. She had lived a happy life because she had identified the things that made her so insecure. She had named her enemies and did not let them have the victory over her but told them No. Most of all, she knew the deep and abiding love of God.

Just because birth order influenced your personality, you can't let it be your excuse all your life. "I'm so shy because I was a middle child," or "I'm so driven because I was a first child" may be true statements about you, but they don't have to be written in stone. The driven person can slow down; the shy person can step out.

One important thing to remember when grappling with the birth-order problem: If your older sibling has firstborn problems, and your younger sibling has baby-of-the-family problems, then there probably is no ideal order to be born in. Each carries its own advantages and disadvantages, and you can take comfort in the fact that you would not be any better off had you been born somewhere different in the family tree.

2. *Temperament*

At one point in my twenties, I lived with my older sister and her husband. I always thought my older sister and I got along rather well. It wasn't long, however, before we began to realize that there were some real thorny points in our relationship.

Finally her husband decided we needed to sit down and figure out what the problem was. As a minister, he had just taken a course in counseling in which he learned to administer a temperament test. The test was designed for premarital counseling, but he thought it could be valuable in figuring out where the problems were in our relationship.

The test was scored on graphs that illustrated extremes. For example, one scale might be Happy/Sad. On every category, I scored right in the middle, the perfectly balanced temperament. Except for two—and they told the story.

On the Dominant/Submissive test, I nearly went off the graph on the submissive side. And on the graph measuring hostility, there again I almost went off the chart.

I spent a lot of my time being submissive to people, doing things their way so they would like me. Inside, however, festered a deep hostility toward those people for whom I was being a doormat. Not surprisingly, my sister's Dominant/Submissive score was high on the dominant side.

Just finding this clue to my temperament and what made me react the way I did to my sister brought major changes in my life.

I then discovered a whole area of study on the different temperament types that explains so much about personality. You don't need to have a counselor administer a personality test for you. Many books on the market describe and explain the four different personality temperaments. The book I use, and have found very valuable because of its Christian slant, is *Spirit-Controlled Temperament* by Tim LaHaye.

The four major temperament classifications are called sanguine, choleric, melancholy, and phlegmatic. When you learn which describes your personality, a lot can be predicted about how you react and don't react to your life circumstances. No one falls completely under one category, but as you find out more about your personality type, you will come to understand yourself much better.

The problem is, as we grow up, we bring with us the mistaken idea that some personality traits are "normal" or "all right," while others are undesirable. "Jenny's always so positive and optimistic," you say enviously. "Why can't I be more like her?" Unbeknown to you, Jenny is saying, "Joe is such a realist. I wish I had more of that quality instead of being so pie-in-the-sky."

The truth is that each personality type has its own weaknesses and strengths. Once you realize that everyone has some kind of personality deficiency, it does make it easier to accept your own.

For example, I have always been prone to bouts of depression. It helped me immensely to know that this was one characteristic of my temperament type and was not some major flaw in my character. Personality traits of this kind can be changed, or at least modified and controlled. And anyway, I happen to like a lot of the traits I receive from my second personality type.

Learning about middle-child syndrome was a starting

point in my self-discoveries. From there I traveled through my childhood, my teen years, and my young adult years and found the incidents that had made the greatest impact on me. I remembered the young couple from camp asking someone else to ride in their car. A seemingly trivial incident, but I knew it was important because of the emotion it could still stir up inside of me.

Those are the incidents you want to pull out of your memory—the ones that can still cause you to feel embarrassed, hurt, angry, and rejected. As you fit them together into a whole, you will begin to see the patterns into which your life has fallen. For me, I got a clear picture of the submissive/hostile pattern. "Please don't reject me" was written on my every action, followed by a lot of anger as I found myself doing or saying things I never wanted to.

To break a pattern or a habit, you must first know what the pattern is—name the enemy, define the pattern. Then you can go to work on strategies to defeat or change them.

Chapter 3

The Tunnel

I have loved you with an everlasting love.—Jeremiah 31:3,
NASB.

One gorgeous day I decided to take a walk. I had asked
God to come along with me, and He was delighted to do so.
Creation around us sang praises to Him as we walked and
talked.

Along our way, He talked to me about life—my life—and
what it meant to Him. He told me that He had created me
and knew everything there was to know about me. I tried to
listen to what He was saying, especially when He would
point out pitfalls along the way to keep me from stumbling.

But to tell the truth, the day was so beautiful, and there
were just too many things to see and do along the way. His
words played in the background of my mind, but I was
preoccupied with enjoying the day.

Then we came to a hillside. We had come to plenty of
others. Some we had climbed and been exhilarated to reach
the top. Some we had walked around, not quite able to
make the climb. So this hillside didn't seem all that different at first. Then I noticed that a tunnel had been bored
into the rocky side of the hill. I'm not sure how I knew it
was a tunnel, because when I peered into it, all I saw was
darkness. But I was sure it would come out on the other
side of the hill.

Without consulting my companion, I took a step into the
tunnel. He looked at me sadly. "Don't go in there. Stay out

39

here in the light with Me," He said.

I don't remember if I even answered Him. The tunnel was new, something different. In fact, it looked like a place where I would be safe from some of the hurtful things we had encountered on our walk.

Cutting through the tunnel looked a lot easier than having to walk around yet another hill or climbing another mountain. So I stepped in, plunging myself into darkness.

I graduated from high school. A big day! Everyone so sure that life would be full of surprises and wonderful things from that day on. We cried and hugged each other in celebration of leaving childhood behind. We thought that now we were adults, and life was ours for the taking.

Of course, we didn't realize that we had to be willing to reach out and take it. During the next year, I made big plans, and I even made halfhearted attempts to find a better job than the one I had clerking at a dime store. But in truth I wasn't so sure life was mine for the taking. It belonged to those who were smarter, prettier, more outgoing.

At one point a girlfriend and I decided to take an apartment together. We got very excited about the prospect of having our own place on the beach and, as a token of the seriousness of our decision, we went shopping. We filled two carts with things like dishpans and laundry baskets and throw pillows. Everything we would need to set up housekeeping. We put it all on layaway, like a treasure stored up toward our future.

It wasn't long before we stopped talking about it. We never mentioned the things that some poor store clerk had written up for us and found space for in a storeroom. I suppose at some point he realized we were never coming back, and he put the things back on the shelf.

That incident was indicative of my life. I wasn't afraid to dream or even to make big plans. But when it came time to carry through with them, I was afraid. Afraid I would fail, afraid I couldn't handle what I'd decided to take on. And usually my dreams were a desperate attempt to drag myself out of the ordinary and turn my life into something exciting and special. The disappointment of failure would have been more than I could bear.

Nothing seemed to come together that year, and I admitted that I was floundering. I had no idea what to do with my life. So when the opportunity came for my sister and me to live with an aunt and uncle in Washington, D.C., I jumped at the chance.

The big city. Now I had it made. Now I could make trips home and dazzle my friends with what I had become: a sophisticated, self-confident woman of the world.

Instead, I was homesick. My job was boring. My sister had broken up with her fiancé and was moody all summer long. I felt more alone than ever, more unloved than ever. No one cared about me and the big empty hole inside of me that needed love.

The yearning for love and acceptance grew stronger than ever. God couldn't fill the void now because I had begun the process of stepping into the tunnel. I had only one choice: to find a man who would marry me.

Finding a man was going to take care of all the problems facing me. I would no longer have to worry about my lack of ambition or my fear of failing at a career. I wouldn't need a job once I found a man to take care of me. And a man would definitely take care of those feelings of worthlessness. How could a woman not feel valued if someone was willing to commit himself to her for the rest of his life?

I had the common schoolgirl concept of what true love was all about. In someone else's eyes, I would become a treasure. Even when the day came that he got to know the real me, it wouldn't change his mind about loving me. My faults, my weaknesses would all be a part of the reason he loved me so very much. I would live on a pedestal, buoyed through life on this wonderful condition of "true love."

It seems silly now to think I could have been so naïve. But giving up that dream would have been admitting that I had to start facing life on my own, and I couldn't do that.

In this state of mind, I met a man. He was crazy about me. He pursued me, wined me, dined me, and spent every spare moment he had with me. For the first time, I didn't feel awkward or threatened. We would talk for hours about everything under the sun. I really believed I could let him see the real me.

The problem was, I had been wearing a mask for so long, I didn't know how to take it off. I did the things I thought he wanted me to do and tried to be the person I thought he wanted me to be, all the while thinking I was finally having an open and mature relationship.

He wasn't a Christian and didn't care to be, but I decided that didn't really matter. You couldn't have everything. Love was enough. We dated for a year, and halfway through that year I found out he was married, living at home with his wife and three children.

This is when I found out how devastating the damage of the not-good-enoughs had been in my life. When he finally confessed to me about his double life, I didn't hesitate a moment. There was no way I was going to give up the only man who made me feel like I was loved and valued. There on the spot I declared that my love for him was too strong to change. The decision went against everything I had been taught, and the longer we were together and the more I learned about him, the more I saw that everything he stood for was wrong for me. But I could not give him up because I was so fearful he might be the only man in the world who would ever love me.

He was soon divorced, and I married him before the ink was dry on the papers. Now I began to truly relax in our relationship, and slowly the real me started emerging. The real me was a woman who valued family, who wanted a life filled with kids, tradition, and church—the whole thing. My husband thought he knew the real me—an independent party girl always ready for a good time. He was pretty taken aback at the person who emerged after the "I do's" were said.

It lasted for three years. Finally a time came when our

differences drove us so far apart there was no salvaging the relationship. All my hopes that he would eventually come to know God and that together we would find out what it really meant to be Christians came to naught. The longer he was with me, the more he resented the church and what he saw as my hypocritical ways.

One day he was gone. There were sporadic attempts to work things out, but he was happy only when I compromised and did things his way. There was no hope for a meeting of the minds. He left, and with his departure came the incontrovertible truth. I wasn't even good enough to hold on to the man who had vowed to love me forever. The real me was never good enough.

For some reason, this time, I was through trying on my own. Instead of donning my mask once again and going back out into the fray, I bared my soul. All I wanted was for God to come back into my life and give me the peace in my heart that I had had so long before. I didn't know how to get a relationship with God back. Night after night, in the darkness of my bedroom, the tears would come. And night after night I prayed the same prayer: "God, please help me."

The tunnel got darker and darker as I plunged ever deeper. I should have stopped and tried to get my bearings, but it didn't seem possible. It was just too dark, and things just moved too fast.

Inside the darkness, there was no one to protect or love me. Only me. Every moment, the only person I had was me. I was afraid that if I stopped for even a minute, I was going to have to deal with that person. Instead, I kept telling myself that just one more step would bring me to the place in the tunnel that was going to feel like home, the place that was going to make all the ugliness worth stumbling through.

Finally the darkness became unbearable. The memories were dim, but I knew that somewhere outside of that tunnel there had been sunlight and flowers and singing and laughing. There had been someone who had promised to stay with me forever. So I started looking for a way out, a way back to the sunshine.

That's when I came to the end of the tunnel. I saw light ahead, but every step toward it felt mired in quicksand. I seemed to be trapped in the tunnel. "God, please help me!" I cried out over and over, and with every cry, I came closer to the light.

As I stepped outside, relief flooding over me, I saw something so wonderful I could scarcely believe it. God was waiting there at the exit. I had walked away from Him, deserted Him in the middle of a conversation. I had told Him I didn't need His advice; I had rejected Him. But there He was, waiting for me at the end of the tunnel.

He hadn't finished the walk without me.

> What man among you, if he has a hundred sheep and has lost one of them, does not leave the ninety-nine in the open pasture, and go after the one which is lost, until he finds it? And when he has found it, he lays it on his shoulders, rejoicing. And when he comes home, he calls together his friends and his neighbors, saying to them, "Rejoice with me, for I have found my sheep which was lost!" I tell you that in the same way, there will be more joy in heaven over one sinner who repents, than over ninety-nine righteous persons who need no repentance (Luke 15:4-7, NASB).

Have you ever put yourself in the place of that sheep? Have you ever let yourself picture the Lord looking over the sea of humanity and noticing that you—distinct, individual you—were missing? And then imagine Him searching, knowing where you are but maybe not being able to get your attention, persevering, until finally that joyous day comes when He takes you gently on His shoulders and runs home rejoicing. He doesn't finish the walk without you. It doesn't matter how many others He has gathered together for the walk, He wants you there with Him to make His joy complete.

I had certainly never put myself in the place of the lost sheep. I had been so busy hating myself that I just assumed everyone else, including God, felt the same way. Intellectually I knew I was the sheep He had loved enough to come after, because I'm sure more than one preacher had pointed it out to me along the way. But in the picture in my mind, I was one of the ninety-nine, jostling around in the pen, bleating to be recognized.

I realized something astonishing then. I had never thought of myself as an individual before God. The Bible says, "For God so loved the world . . ." and I had never been able to imagine myself standing out as anything special in the sea of humanity that makes up the world. I had a lot to learn about God's love before I would finally be able to love myself.

1. *He loved me enough to die for me.*

There could be no real understanding of the personal love He has for me if there was no understanding of the personal sacrifice He made for me.

> Surely our griefs He Himself bore, and our sorrows He carried; yet we ourselves esteemed Him stricken, smitten of God, and afflicted. But He was pierced through for our transgressions, He was crushed for our iniquities; the chastening for our well-being fell upon Him, and by His scourging we are healed. All of us like sheep have gone astray, each of us has turned to his own way; but the Lord has caused the iniquity of us all to fall on Him (Isaiah 53:4-6, NASB).

I remember once hearing a preacher talk about the crucifixion. It was the last night of a week at Bible camp, and he was pulling out all the stops to get the gospel across to us before we got on our buses and went home the next morning. He told the story step by step, in gruesome detail. When he came to the part where the soldier pounded the nails into Jesus' hands and feet, the preacher began to pound on the pulpit, slowly and rhythmically, simulating the sound the hammer would have made. As he finished his sermon, he continued pounding, letting the harsh sound bring home to us the reality of Jesus' physical sacrifice.

I hadn't really "heard" that sermon then, but finally, years later, the pounding fist echoed in my mind. For the first time, I became overwhelmed with the enormity of the sacrifice Jesus had made to save me *because He loved me.*

2. *He knows me individually.*

Jesus' sacrifice was not made for the faceless millions. If that had been the case, the shepherd would not have needed to go after the one lost sheep. The multitude in the pasture would have been sufficient, because the one would not even have been missed. But He had missed *me* and come after *me.* I was important to Him as an individual; He knew my face in the crowd.

" 'Are not five sparrows sold for two cents? And yet not one of them is forgotten before God. Indeed, the very hairs of your head are all numbered. Do not fear; you are of more value than many sparrows' " (Luke 12:6, 7, NASB). These verses are so familiar that we miss the wonderful way they apply to us.

In Sunday school we had been taught the three attributes of God: omniscience, omnipotence, and omnipresence. And if God was omniscient, of course He knew how many hairs there were on my head. What else was new? I had missed the point. I had seen the big picture—the power of God—but I had not seen the whole picture—the gentle love of God. He had not only loved me, *He had taken the time to get to know me individually.*

3. *God delights in His relationship with me.*

Zephaniah 3:17 says, "The Lord thy God in the midst of thee is mighty; he will save, he will rejoice over thee with joy; he will rest in his love, he will joy over thee with singing."

Once God had brought me home to the flock, He hadn't

left me there and gone after someone else. Mistakenly, I had viewed Christianity as more of a chore than a relationship. My reasoning went something like this: Now I'm saved, I guess I had better behave so He will keep loving me. Or so He will keep taking care of me. Or so He won't be sorry He ever bothered with me in the first place.

I had struggled with the rules in a desperate attempt to earn the love He had already given me, because no one ever told me about Zephaniah 3:17. He didn't want my life with Him to be a chore. A challenge, yes, so that I would continue to move forward. But more than that, He wanted me to be His friend. He was singing over me with joy! *God took delight in our relationship*!

Leaving the tunnel and finding Jesus waiting for me had changed my entire perspective. I had believed that, from beginning to end, the Christian life was meant to be one long struggle. Christians just had to put their heads down, grit their teeth, and try to move forward. I thought the great hope of all Christians lay in how many jewels they would find in the crowns they received in glory or in how big their mansions would be.

Now I knew that I had already received the reward—God was my friend. In the end, every human being in my life had failed to give me the total, unconditional acceptance I had needed. When I had slapped my girlfriend across the face those many years before, she did not speak to me for weeks. And even when she finally did speak to me, she was never my friend again.

I had done a lot more than slap God's face—I had rejected Him the way I feared He was going to reject me. Was it like the uniform? Like my career aspirations? If I rejected Him first and didn't try to live up to the list of rules, then I wouldn't have to suffer the hurt of His rejection.

When that rejection didn't come, even after the terrible way I had treated Him, it started me on a new course. While I finally understood that I had value, that I was truly loved, it would still be many years before I learned to love myself.

Chapter 4

Fear of Rejection

I don't know of another emotion [rejection] that is so often exploited by demonic powers. Overwhelmed by their rejections, people cannot seem to break out of their shells.—Erwin Lutzer.

"If only I were pretty, he wouldn't have left me." The words hung in the air, taunting me. I knew as I spoke them that they were ridiculous, but the little voice inside kept probing: "Are they ridiculous? Can you really be sure that it wouldn't have made any difference if you had been a little prettier, a little smarter?"

Gaining some self-esteem was a long process. I had spent a lifetime perfecting my habits and response patterns. It made sense that I was going to have to learn a whole new way of handling things.

To be honest, before taking the temperament test with my brother-in-law, I had never stopped to analyze what motivated me as a person, why I was the way I was. I really had no idea what a submissive, fearful person I had become. Rejection avoidance had become so ingrained in me that I didn't realize I could be any other way. Whether I acted out in anger, fear, or passivity, every emotion resulted from wanting desperately to be accepted and being afraid that I wasn't. Fear of rejection motivated nearly everything I did during my twenties, but of course I couldn't have stated it so clearly then. At the time, all I knew was that life hurt, and nobody seemed to care much.

49

Finding and recognizing God's love was a first step, but that old disease, the not-good-enoughs, plagued me constantly. That little voice constantly taunted me with thoughts like, "If you were only prettier, only smarter, only a better conversationalist, only a better anything . . ." If it could make me believe in some shortcoming, that shortcoming became real.

I laugh now at some of the ridiculous things I did while trying to avoid rejection. On one occasion, my roommate and I decided to have a party. Before committing to it, however, I took a poll among my friends. "Would you come if I invited you to a party?" I asked each one. Only when enough of them had answered in the affirmative did I have the courage to actually plan the party.

Another instance occurred after I had moved to the "big city" and had my own apartment. During one of my visits to my family, a young man stopped by to see us. It just so happened that this man had once broken my heart, rejecting me for another young woman. So now, as we chatted, I kept waiting for some sign from him that he was now impressed with my new independence, maybe some sign that he regretted having chosen that other woman over me.

When that sign was not forthcoming, I decided to try eliciting the response I wanted. So I blurted out, "I bet you never expected to see me with my own apartment and living in the big city!" I don't remember his exact response. I know he didn't say, "Wow, you're right; you're really something!" But I do remember his response was accompanied by a not-very-affirming smirk. In my desperate attempt to force him into showing me approval, I had only succeeded in compounding the rejection.

Incidents like these can be amusing, but in the prologue I told about an incident in which my fear of rejection nearly led me to make a morally harmful choice. The sum of these choices created a lifestyle based on fear of rejection, and bad choices had become a standard response for me.

A group of friends once made up a list of things they had

done in the name of rejection avoidance. The long list contained both trivial and important items. The trivial items included pretending to hold a political view opposite to his own so the person would feel more accepted by the others in the room; laughing along with a group of people at a television preacher, even though he really liked and respected the preacher; taking a long walk with someone and never mentioning that her shoes were killing her, afraid that she would somehow be diminished in her companion's eyes.

The list moved on, however, to the more important items. Years of always giving in had taken their toll, and the trivial compromises became bigger as one talked of drinking to fit in, even though alcohol made her nauseated; another spoke of smoking pot, even though the "high" that it produced frightened him; and more than one woman admitted to compromising her values when dating in order to get men to call back a second time.

Fear of rejection, just like any other fear, holds its victims in bondage. Often the ones suffering feel that they are no longer in control of their lives as they make decisions that bring only unhappiness. An understanding of what rejection really is goes a long way in relieving that fear.

What so many of us fail to realize is that rejection is inevitable. If our lives are lived solely to find acceptance and avoid rejection, we will fail. Even an active, healthy, functioning adult faces rejection nearly every day of his or her life. Accepting rejection as an inevitable part of living is vital to being released from a bondage of fear.

The word *rejection* carries a lot of subliminal baggage, all of it negative. The word automatically brings to mind the "Dear John" letter. Whether it's related to our jobs, our homes, our friends, or our churches, we equate rejection with being "dumped on."

Actually, rejection can be a purely practical decision that has no personal bearing on our value as a human being. At times rejection is merely the result of deciding between several available options.

No one—not the most beautiful, sought-after actress; not

the most self-assured, charismatic politician; not the most well-loved minister—can avoid rejection. It's a fact of life. Applicants for a job have to accept the fact that only one person can be chosen. Actors auditioning for a role know that their chances of being rejected are greater than their chances of being hired. A writer understands that rejection is a part of the job description.

We all will be rejected some of the time. When my eight-year-old raises her hand in the classroom along with ten other students, only one of them will be called on. This is a form of rejection. Some of those children perceive it as personal rejection. "The teacher doesn't like me—she never calls on me." Others try again the next time, patiently waiting for it to become their turn to be called on.

This is what I call "practical" rejection. Someone makes a choice between A and B. Someone tries to choose the very best candidate, as when hiring a person to fill a position. Sometimes one chooses randomly, as when a teacher selects one of many children to give an answer to the question.

The other kind of rejection is "personal" rejection; that's the kind in which our fears are rooted. Occasionally some people make a choice based on not liking B, so they take A, no matter what. They are rejecting B, not choosing A. Personally, I believe that this type of rejection occurs a lot less often than the other.

It was imperative for me to learn the difference between personal and practical rejection. People inflicted with the not-good-enoughs have a particularly hard time distinguishing between the two. Every rejection, no matter what form it takes, gives proof to our worst fear—we truly are unworthy or unlovable.

But it is possible to learn the difference between practical and personal rejection. The process does take a little time but can become second nature if practiced enough. The trick is to take the rejection and analyze it, going beyond the emotional conclusions that we reach upon the first sting of the rejection.

How do we do that? The only way is to be able to step

back and take an objective look at the event. Until we can do that, we will never have a clear picture of what is actually happening in our lives. Our fear of rejection is so overwhelming that we see only ourselves and the hurt that has been inflicted. We must be able to distance ourselves from that hurt if we are to have a rational view of rejection.

Years ago, a woman began attending the church to which I belonged. After knowing her a short while, I sensed that we had a lot in common, and I felt drawn to her. I began to cultivate our friendship, inviting her to lunch and showing her around town. But instead of our friendship growing as I had hoped, she suddenly hit it off with another woman. To add to the insult, this other woman didn't even appear to have much in common with her. I reacted immediately the way I always had, moping around and feeling sorry for myself, thoroughly convinced that I was a social outcast. "I'm not likable. That other woman is prettier/smarter/funnier than I am." I was down in the dumps for quite a while over this perceived rejection.

What could I have learned about this rejection if I had taken the time to analyze it? For one thing, I would have remembered that forming friendships is an almost mystical thing. Who can ever tell why two people hit it off when they seem so obviously mismatched? Look at the close friendships in your life. Did you go out and choose those people, then make them into your friends? Or did the circumstances of life bring you together more and more, until over time you formed a bond?

Examined objectively, the woman did not reject my friendship. Circumstances led her in another direction, into different friendships. Had I not always been so ready to put myself down, I could have recognized it as simply the disappointment it was and gotten on with my life.

The rejection was practical, not personal. She did not reject me as a person, because we did remain friends, even if not as close as I had hoped. She simply was drawn to someone else and moved naturally in that direction.

Another thing I would have recognized was that I did

have other friendships that needed my time and attention. The best response to a rejection, personal or practical, is action. Had I turned my attention to those who did want my company and needed my caring touch, my injured ego would have been built back up by their positive feedback. I shouldn't have taken time to dwell on something I couldn't change anyway.

Let's look at some other examples of rejection. First, identify whether they are practical or personal. Then think about the various possible responses and decide which ones will have the more positive effect. Last, choose some kind of action you can take to lessen the sting of the rejection.

Example one: The company you've always wanted to work for has just advertised an opening. You apply immediately, but someone else gets the job.

Identify the rejection. Were you denied the job because they didn't like you (personal) or because someone else had better qualifications (practical)?

Response one: I knew I wouldn't get it. I don't come across well at interviews. I probably would have done an awful job even if I had gotten the position.

Response two: The other applicant must have been a little better qualified than I am. I'll have to try again if they have another opening.

Action to take: If, after honest examination, you really do think you did a poor job with the interview, sharpen your interviewing skills. Get a friend to work with you. Improve your appearance if need be. Read some of the books that tell how to make a good impression at an interview.

You may, however, come to the conclusion that the opening was filled on the basis of the applicant's qualifications and had nothing to do with you personally. After all, you probably were not the only person rejected for the job. In that case, take some positive action to make yourself better qualified. Improve your skills or take some courses to widen your knowledge. Get an advanced degree if that will help. And by all means, try again. Don't ever let a rejection keep you from going after your dreams.

They say that the best revenge is a life well lived. If you want to show the not-good-enoughs that they can't get you down, do the very best job you can in the position you are currently holding. Be the best you can be, wherever you are.

Example two: You've entered a writing contest held by a magazine in which you've always wanted to be published. The response comes back: "The choice was hard to make, as we received over 4,500 entries. We are sorry yours didn't make it, but thank you for your effort."

Identify the rejection: Was your manuscript rejected because evaluators didn't like your writing (personal), or was it rejected because someone else's article was more what they were looking for (practical)?

Response one: I knew I wouldn't win. Why do I set myself up for rejection by entering stupid contests like that? They probably hated my manuscript. What have I got to say that anyone would want to read anyway?

Response two: Over four thousand entries! Well, maybe mine was the second best, you never know. And anyway, 4,498 other people got rejected right along with me. Now, what is another magazine that likes this kind of article?

Action to take: Is your writing as good as it can be? If your article was rejected because the writing was bad, improve your writing. Take a creative writing course from your local adult-education program or from one of the many correspondence courses that are offered. Let someone read your writing and make suggestions on how you can improve it.

Learn how to write for specific markets. If you are sending articles about child care to a magazine for seniors, you should expect rejection. Read, read, read, practice, practice, practice, until you understand your markets and what it is you really want to accomplish with your writing.

Was the article well-written but just not the best of the lot? See if you can find ways to improve it; then submit it elsewhere—fast, before you lose your confidence. I've heard tales of well-known authors who submitted manuscripts for years before finding the right publisher.

Example three: Most of your family members live in Texas, except for one sister, who is in Colorado, and you, who live in New Jersey. When it comes time to plan vacations, the Texas siblings almost always choose the Colorado sister, and you're feeling pretty left out in New Jersey.

Identify the rejection: Are they choosing Colorado because they don't like visiting you (personal), or is Colorado closer and cheaper (practical)?

Response one: Nancy is their favorite sister. They've always liked her best. No one cares about seeing me.

Response two: It's a lot more expensive for them to come to New Jersey than to visit Colorado. They can drive to one and have to fly to the other. There's also a lot more to see and do in Colorado. I guess if I lived in Texas, I'd visit Colorado more often too, since I could get more for my time and money. Anyway, several of them have been to visit me, which shows that they wanted to see me in spite of the distance.

Action to take: One aspect of learning to respect yourself more is letting people know your feelings. Let your family know that this has been a sore spot for you but also that you understand the reasons. This way, they might make a bit more effort to visit you, or at the very least do other things that will let you know you are loved and valued.

Get the whole family involved in vacation planning. One way to reduce the cost is to have everyone travel to a location halfway between the two. As you and other family members get involved in finding creative ways of getting together, you will be better able to see how economics and not sibling favoritism has limited their visits to you.

We cannot avoid rejection. What we can do is learn to live with it and lessen its effect on our self-esteem.

While still learning to evaluate the different situations of rejection you encounter, it might be a good idea to actually sit down and write out an analysis just as I've done here: the situation, type of rejection, response one, response two, and action to take. In this way, you learn to think analytically rather than to respond emotionally, and eventually it becomes easier to assess the situation automatically.

Chapter 5

Lessons Along the Way

Do not think of yourself more highly than you ought, but rather think of yourself with sober judgment.—Romans 12:3, NIV.
Satan, the master of extremes, wants us either to deify ourselves or degrade ourselves.—Randy and Nanci Alcorn.

1. Helping Others

"If God didn't want us to have sex before we get married, then why did He give me these feelings?" Wanda was sixteen, and she was very serious about the question.

After my divorce, I had packed up everything that would fit into my little Pinto station wagon and moved to St. Louis to live with my older sister and her husband. He was a youth minister at the time, and I began to spend a lot of my time as a counselor for his female teens.

The girls also became my friends. They trusted me enough to bring me their private, difficult questions. "Why shouldn't I marry a non-Christian if I'm really in love with him?" "What's wrong with a little fooling around on a date as long as I don't go too far?" "How do you know when you're in love?"

I discovered that the kids in the youth group really liked me and enjoyed my company. Besides having a lot of fun working with them, I was gaining something for myself—a little self-esteem. Dedicating so much of my time and effort to them was actually helping me.

This was one of the many lessons I learned by accident

as I blundered through life. Giving of ourselves to help others actually can be good for our own self-esteem. When we are hurting, we turn inward so much that we lose perspective. Once I turned my focus outward, spending less time thinking about myself, I began to receive some of the love and positive affirmation I needed.

For one thing, I saw that I could make a difference in someone's life, that there was something special I had to give. I had a talent, an ability to communicate with the teens without being judgmental or talking down to them. After all I had been through, I had answers for these kids that could possibly help them avoid some of the pitfalls along the way.

I put all of my energies into working with the youth group and loved every minute of it. Another reward in working with teens was that I found them to be less threatening than adults. They loved me and showed their love openly—something I desperately needed.

People with poor self-images never think they have anything to contribute. They feel worthless, without value. That feeling varies in intensity from person to person, but it is always present. Of course I was familiar with the passage in 1 Corinthians 12 stating that we are all part of the body and that all the parts are necessary to make the body function. But I didn't feel my part was very important— possibly a toenail or maybe even an appendix. Nothing of any great significance that you just couldn't live without.

You will never discover your significance if you are not doing anything for the body. If you are spending your life taking care of yourself, always fearful to be an active member of the body, you might just as well be dead cells. But once you reach out, once you begin to work actively for the good of the body, you begin to feel like a real part of a living organism.

There are so many ways in which we can help others. It is important to find an area in which we feel we really are being effective; otherwise, we will only give ourselves more ammunition to feed the not-good-enoughs. ("See, I can't even succeed at volunteer work!")

For me, it was working with teens. An older friend of mine has a ministry to the shut-in members of our church. She writes to them and sends them the weekly bulletin from the worship service. They have come to look forward to her cheerful notes and to think of her as their friend and a link to the church they can no longer physically attend. At the same time, this ministry makes her feel needed and loved.

Outside of the church, other organizations help people in need. Maybe you don't really want to work in a soup kitchen, but how about working a few hours a week at a Salvation Army store. One friend of mine goes to the elementary school once a week to read or do projects with the special-needs students. The children love her, and some even call her Grandma.

One church I attended was within walking distance of a small nursing home. When Carly, a resident of that home, began attending services at our church, a woman in the congregation started offering her rides. Those rides turned into occasional lunch dates, and now she takes Carly shopping once a week to buy her toiletries and personal items. She has virtually adopted Carly. How many others could use a friend like that?

Some people call it ministry; others just call it "helping others." Whatever you call it, it still means the same thing. You are utilizing the gifts that God gave you as a special member of His body. Through the years, I have put my gifts to use in various ways. Today I no longer work with teens, but I am always searching for the place where my particular talents can be put to good use.

This principle has always proven true. I am happiest when I focus on someone else's needs rather than on my own.

2. Forming Friendships

Sometimes I'm amazed that I was ever able to form any close friendships. I was very timid about approaching others. I never liked to ask someone to do something with me, such as going out to eat or going shopping, because I didn't want to have to watch them as they tried to come up with an excuse not to go.

Even now I prefer dealing with people over the phone. In fact, it wasn't long ago that I wanted to ask a friend to go with me to a Christian Women's Club luncheon. It was going to be my first time speaking at one of the luncheons, and I wanted to have someone along for moral support.

I called Beth. With great relief, I heard her message machine answer. Message machines are easy to handle; they treat everyone the same. I left a message, saying, "Beth, I'll go ahead and ask you this on your answering machine so you'll have time to think of a reason to say No before you call me back. You wouldn't want to go . . . ," etc.

I might as well have come right out and said, "Hi, Beth. I'm sorry it's me bothering you. I know you would rather be talking to anyone else. Though this event is really important to me, I can't imagine why that should matter to you. Just say No, and let's get this over with. I'll never bother you again, I promise."

When Beth returned my call, she said, "We have to work on this attitude of yours. Of course I would love to go with you!"

Psychologists remind us that just by wording a request inappropriately, we can invite people to say No and reject us. We have to resist the tendency to phrase invitations negatively: "You probably wouldn't want to go out to eat with me, would you?" "I know you're busy and don't have time, so just say No."

So there are two major ways in which the not-good-enoughs limit us in forming friendships: (1) We are afraid to ask people to do things with us and invite them in a negative manner that encourages them to reject the invitation; or (2) we are so afraid of their rejection that we don't even invite them in the first place.

I will admit that I'm much better about taking the initiative in relationships now. Even though I worry about rejection, I don't let it stop me anymore. That's where I've changed over the years. I pursue a friendship now even when I'm frightened. Lots of times I fall on my face, but I still think it's worth taking the risk and making the effort.

Another thing I have learned to do is to surround myself with people who will give me positive affirmation. Part of forming healthy friendships means finding people you trust to give you their honest opinions—good and bad—loving you enough to care. Avoid negative people or people who like to manipulate and control. An extreme example of this is women who stay in abusive relationships because they don't think they deserve any better. We do deserve better. It's all right to have someone tell you once in a while that you are special.

3. Dating Relationships

Finally I started dating again. That was almost enough to put me back at square one.

In male/female relationships, more than anywhere else, the need for total acceptance blinds us. It is so easy to lose our perspective and start basing our self-worth on whether the cute guy in our psychology class asks us out. It seemed that the men I was attracted to were always attracted to someone else and that someone else was invariably prettier and more sophisticated than I was. My self-esteem began to take a nose dive again as I waited for some handsome "prince charming" to take notice of me.

Then finally the cute guy in my night-school psychology class did ask me out, and it seemed as though there really was hope. We were always making each other laugh in class, and whenever we had problems with classwork we would help each other out. I felt very relaxed with him and was very excited about our date.

He took me to a nice restaurant, and everything seemed perfect. Except that suddenly I didn't have the faintest idea what to say to him. I'm sure he must have wondered where the happy-go-lucky, talkative woman he sat next to in class had gone. I knew where she was; I was just so afraid of saying or doing the wrong thing that I held her deep inside.

I have a friend whose not-good-enoughs manifested themselves in extreme shyness. She went on a blind date once and never said a word to the guy all evening. She liked him, but he never knew it. Instead, he figured she didn't find him attractive in the least. Is it any wonder guys don't call back after an agonizing evening like that? After all, their self-esteem is also on the line.

For me, the problem was that I always expected to be jilted. No matter how well the relationship might be going, I still had that crazy fear of letting the real me come through. I just knew that once a man discovered the real me, he would take off.

When I began dating my future husband, I was certainly watching for signs that he was being unfaithful. I could never quite believe that this handsome, intelligent man was honestly madly in love with me. If I had the slightest suspicion, I would question him accusingly until I could satisfy myself that nothing was wrong.

Finally one day, he said, "Do you know how much it hurts me that you don't trust me? What have I ever done to make you feel that way?"

I guess I had never thought about it. I had lived a certain way for so long that I didn't even realize how I was behaving. I had not realized, until the day he confronted me, that I lived my life expecting rejection and trying to keep my protective mechanisms in good running order.

I had almost driven my future husband away. By trying so hard to protect myself from rejection, I had almost *caused* him to reject me!

4. Motherhood

Motherhood is another place where I have had to fight the not-good-enoughs. Picture a woman with her first baby. She has never known anything so pure and unselfish as the love she feels for this creature. And even more wonderful, for the first time in her life, she is on the receiving end of unconditional love.

Unconditional love—what she hoped to find in her husband, but didn't. Finally, at long last, another human being loves her just for being her. Nothing she does is wrong, because she is Mommy.

Then one day that beautiful little creature reaches the age of two. Mommy is no longer the most wonderful thing in the world, but rather she has become the one who is keeping baby from being all that he would be. Now it is necessary to break away from Mommy and the apron strings and become a person of his own.

Mommy is back where she started, wondering where the person is who will love her unconditionally. Of course, if she is smart, she has kept her perspective and knows that God is the only One who can do that. However, I wasn't smart. I had four babies in less than six years, and it wasn't until after the fourth that it all caught up with me. Until that time, all I could see were the sweet infants I was bringing home, surrounding myself with more love than I had ever thought existed.

Somewhere along the way, I had lost sight of God again. Oh, not of my faith. My faith seemed stronger than ever as I witnessed the miracle of birth. What I lost sight of was that my value came from God and His grace and not from anything around me. Everything had taken a subtle shift as I tried to find my value and my identity in my children.

Do you know what a terrible burden that placed on my children? I wanted them to make me feel special, to give my life meaning, but it wasn't happening. Instead, the older they got, the less they appreciated anything I did. The more rejected I felt, the angrier I became. Depression set in as I realized that I was failing yet again. I had thought I would be the perfect mother, and now I wasn't sure I even liked my children!

In my book *Sometimes I Don't Like My Kids*, I detail how God took me through this depression. He taught me a lot of things about mothering, but the most important thing I had to get straight was my focus. Whenever it moves off Him and starts looking elsewhere to find worth and value, I fall flat on my face. My kids can't give it to me, my husband can't, my friends can't. If I don't know I have value as a child of God, I'm in trouble.

5. Growing Up

This may sound simplistic, but part of the battle against the not-good-enoughs can be won by growing up. I was going to say it can be won by getting older, but that's not the same thing as growing up.

When I was approaching my fortieth birthday, I went through the typical midlife crisis. I wasn't young anymore and thought that life had passed me by. All that was left was the slow decline into old age and then on into death. That's getting older.

But then I grew up. I took note of the women around me and what they were doing with their lives. A sixty-year-old grandmother had finally taken up painting, something she had wanted to do all her life. She was turning out some beautiful work and loving every minute of it.

A friend in her forties got an M.B.A. Another in her fifties was becoming a public speaker, even though she had been terrified of public speaking all her life. These women were living for today, taking each moment they had, and making it into something special. They weren't getting older, they were growing up.

6. Everybody's Got Something

I'm not the greatest of housekeepers. I would say I'm terrible, but luckily I do know people who are worse than I am. Of course, that hasn't stopped me from beating myself over the head with it, seeing it as yet one more area in which I am totally inadequate.

We all have at least one friend who lives inside House Beautiful. Nothing is ever out of place in her home no matter what time of day or night you happen to drop in. You can drop in without calling ahead, because she never has anything to be embarrassed about.

It was all right with me that my friend Lisa was a perfect housekeeper. It didn't bother me that her kitchen counters sparkled constantly as though nothing ever happened in that room. After all, Lisa's kids were teenagers, and I reasoned that with teenagers, it must be possible to regain control of your home.

But then there was Kristin. Kristin upset me. She had four children, the youngest only five. Kristin made me feel like the lowest of life forms every time I saw her beautiful, spotless home. It only made matters worse when I would hear her casually mention her five-year-old making his bed before going to preschool. Making his bed? You can imagine how inadequate I felt with Kristin around.

One day I said something about my terrible housekeeping. Kristin just shook her head and said, "Oh, I wish I weren't so obsessive about cleaning. Sometimes I drive myself crazy with it, and I know I drive the kids crazy."

For some reason, Kristin had grown up with an obsessive need to keep things perfect around her. Maybe that was the way she felt she would gain approval. Or maybe that was the only way she felt she had control over at least one area of her life. I don't know Kristin's reasons. All I know is this: Kristin was as turned off by her obsessive housekeeping as I was by my lack of housekeeping. I had set her up as my idol, my role model, and she wasn't any happier than I was!

Everybody's got some area of discontent in his or her life. Don't ever look at the people around you and think, "They have it all together. I'm the only misfit in the room." Everyone is displeased with something in his or her life and tries to hide it. *Everyone!*

Chapter 6

Hurting Others

Honor one another above yourselves.—Romans 12:10, NIV.
[Some Christians] have difficulty "honoring others" because they feel in need of honor themselves.—Gene A. Getz.

In the next two chapters, I'm going to introduce you to three people. We have all probably known someone like them or even have done similar things ourselves. We'll use these new friends to help us analyze our own insecurities—to show us something about the effects on those around us and to help us learn techniques for overcoming them.

MARGARET. She has gone out of her way to introduce herself to Sandy, the new woman in her mother's support group. Sandy is bright and friendly, and Margaret feels very attracted to her. Even though Margaret is not nearly as outgoing as Sandy, she has discovered through conversations that they have a lot in common. After weeks of building up her courage, Margaret finally asks Sandy to her house for lunch. Sandy explains a previous commitment and declines. Margaret nurses her hurt over what she considers further proof that people don't really like her all that much, and she never invites Sandy again.

JEANNIE. While sitting in Bible study week after week listening to the other women discuss the insights God has given them about particular scriptures, Jeannie will sometimes think of an experience or an insight of her own that is relevant to the conversation. But in the end she can't bring herself to contribute. Somewhere deep inside Jeannie feels she is no good at expressing herself and doesn't really have anything worthwhile to say. Besides, she doesn't think she has studied the Bible long enough to be able to make truly intelligent statements about it.

JIM. So overworked at church that he has almost burned out, Jim is on more committees than he can name. He also teaches an adult Bible class, sings in the choir, and now has agreed to serve the retirees' luncheon. He is growing frustrated and resentful at the way people use him, but he just can't say No. After all, he reasons, people won't like him if he won't help out.

Is it possible that, while we worry about what others think of us, we actually have a negative impact on them that we don't even realize? Back to our friends in a minute. Right now, consider the following story.

My friend Rita was nervously watching her four-year-old. We had been invited to another child's birthday bash, and the mothers were standing on the sidelines observing the festivities.

Finally Rita turned to me and said, "I've been nervous about this party for days, wondering how Jennifer will do with the other kids. I want so much for her to have a good time and get right in there where the action is. But then I ask myself, How can I hope for her to be like that with the example her own mother sets?"

Rita's statement illustrates the two ways that others are affected by our poor self-image when we allow it to control us: (1) We pass our negative personality traits on to those who use us as role models. (2) We ignore or neglect the needs of others because we are overwhelmed with our own hurts or inadequacies.

Before becoming a mother, Rita thought that she was the only one affected by her not-good-enoughs. Now she was finding out that wasn't true. The techniques we employ to shield ourselves from rejection touch everyone who is close to us. Rita was concerned that her attitude was having a negative effect on her little girl.

We often think that our self-image is only our problem—no one else's. But our self-image does affect other people. When we say we have no worth, no value, our entire focus is turned selfward. Self is the most important thing in our lives.

Somewhere along the way, self-esteem disappears, and self-pity takes its place. A person mired in self-pity is rarely concerned with the problems of others because his or her own problems seem too overwhelming. Tim LaHaye, in *Spirit-Controlled Temperament*, says, "The sin of self-pity is so subtle that we do not often recognize it for what it is." Most people suffering with low self-esteem would be shocked were they to be accused of wallowing in self-pity.

Do your thoughts gravitate around "me": Will they like me? Will they laugh at me? Will I fail? Will I look less than perfect?

Sometimes fear crowds concern or caring for others out of one's mind. After all, it is "others" who are causing the pain, "others" who are causing life to be so miserable. In effect, "others" have become the enemy.

More often, however, "others" are left out because there simply is no room, no time for caring about someone else when "me" needs so much attention. Ironically, the person who dislikes himself has, at the same time, placed himself in the position of most importance. The attention he gives himself might be negative, but it still consumes his time and energy.

What are the results of this inward focusing? Obviously, the people around us, even the ones we most want to please, are being hurt. For Rita, it was her little girl. Because she held back timidly even in casual relationships, she was very likely teaching that same timidity to her daughter.

Some inward focusing is valuable—even necessary. Only by knowing ourselves and understanding our problems can we seek the proper healing. But an excess of inward focusing turns into a kind of selfishness. It consumes us as we spend our time in incessant self-examination, relating the events of the day to ourselves, giving them importance only in how they affected our own lives.

Fortunately, it is possible to dig out of the pit of self-pity and learn to turn our focus outward. First, we must learn to distinguish between inward and outward focus. Second, we must admit that we have actually hurt others with our own fear and self-protective behavior.

Let's go back to the three new friends we met at the beginning of this chapter. These people obviously suffered from the not-good-enoughs. They have a lot in common, even though their not-good-enoughs manifest themselves in different ways. Let's take a little closer look to learn what we can from them.

For clarity, let me define a couple of terms. Earlier I spoke about inward focusing. Below, when I use the term *inward*, it refers to the results of negative inward focusing. *Inward* will show us how we hurt *ourselves* when we wallow in the not-good-enoughs. *Outward* is the term I use to describe how we affect *others* with our negative self-image.

First we met Margaret, who took another woman's negative response to a lunch invitation as a flat, good-for-eternity rejection. What can we see really happening here as a result of her insecurities?

Inward: Margaret is going to be alone because she's afraid to extend herself more than once to make a new friend. She will also be more convinced than ever that people don't really like her, thereby making it ever more difficult for her to believe in herself. This is the part we usually see when we look at someone with insecurities. But we frequently fail to recognize the harm being done to others who interact with the insecure person.

Outward: Whether Margaret believes it or not, other women could use and benefit from Margaret's friendship. Possibly the woman who couldn't come for lunch had been looking forward to getting to know Margaret better and was genuinely sorry that she had to turn down this first invitation. Perhaps she was new in the neighborhood and lonely. Maybe she was struggling with a problem that Margaret could help her through.

In fact, she probably said something like, "Let's try again some other time," but Margaret had already started her self-pity trip and tuned her out. Maybe the other woman was truly bewildered when Margaret seemingly cooled toward her.

Most likely we could add several other ways that Margaret has hurt others. This analysis is valuable if it makes us more aware of the true consequences of our actions.

Let's look at Jeannie, the woman who is afraid to share at her Bible study. She has many reasons for her fear: She doesn't know the Bible as well as the others in the group. She isn't good at expressing herself. She usually puts her foot in her mouth. She . . . well, obviously a lot of inward focusing is going on here.

Now let's imagine that Jeannie's group is discussing a passage of Scripture, and gradually the discussion veers off in the wrong direction. Jeannie has studied the passage before and has some insights on it that could set the discussion on the right track. What happens here when she is too timid to speak up?

Inward: Jeannie has, of course, reinforced within herself that it's better not to speak out. Every time she gives in to her fears, she reinforces them and makes it increasingly difficult to make a change the next time. She will probably go home wishing she had said something, mulling over the situation for days. She will also miss out on the positive feedback and encouragement she would have gotten from the other women had she spoken out.

Outward: The other women leave the class without understanding what the Bible is saying to them in that particular passage.

We can imagine Jeannie in other scenarios. Maybe a woman in the group is suffering through a problem—divorce, a rebellious teenager, lack of enthusiasm for spiritual matters—and needs to hear that Jeannie has suffered through a similar problem and triumphed. Or just that Jeannie is suffering along with her so that she is not alone. Jeannie deprives others of both her insight and her support when she holds back.

Then we come to Jim, saying Yes to anything anyone asks of him and resenting everyone. At first glance, it appears that everyone is taking advantage of Jim, but let's see what is really happening.

Inward: We already know that Jim is a walking time bomb of hostility. Someday he's going to explode, probably at his family, since he can't bring himself to be honest anywhere else. He's allowed himself to be put in a situation where he feels stressed all the time. No matter how much he blames others for putting him there, it was ultimately he who allowed it. In addition, he's setting himself up for ulcers or some other stress-related health problem.

Outward: People always go to Jim because Jim will say Yes. They probably think of Jim as a good worker, someone who likes to be involved. They would be shocked and deeply hurt to find out how much Jim resents them.

Also, because Jim is so easy to persuade, they feel no need to come up with other names to help with the project or use creativity to explore other ways of handling it.

Still other people might be hurt by Jim's inability to say No. In the congregation are people too timid to volunteer but waiting eagerly to be needed. No one will ever ask them if Jim is grudgingly doing it all.

Most important, Jim's family is being hurt. They suffer from his dark moods and outbursts of temper; they also suffer from his lack of time for them.

It's no secret that God created something very complex when He came up with human beings. It would be naïve to suggest simple answers to the problems we are discussing here. But a few guidelines can help. Inward focusing is safe when balanced with adequate outward focusing.

Only when it becomes impossible for us to see, or care, about our effect on those around us, when it results in self-pity instead of self-improvement, is inward focusing dangerous.

Chapter 7

Pretending

As he thinks within himself, so he is.—**Proverbs 23:7, NASB.**

After you analyze your behavior and fears through a balance of inward and outward focusing, what do you do next? You now understand yourself—at least slightly. What do you do to make your perspective practical?

Even though you just finished taking a realistic look at yourself, you now need to start pretending. Yes, pretending. But this pretending is not an escape from the not-good-enoughs. It is a way to start dealing with them. Some counselors jestingly refer to the process as "fake it till you make it." But a certain type of pretending is part of a process that develops confidence.

Psychologists explain it this way: If you act confident—even though you feel not-good-enough inside—most of the time people will reward you by treating you the way you would like (not the way the not-good-enoughs have trained you to expect). When you continue to pretend you are confident again and again, the positive feedback will chip away at the not-good-enoughs. After a while you will begin to feel confident; your feelings will start to match your actions. The pretended gradually becomes real.

Let's call back our three friends from the previous chapter to help us see how this process works. First we had Margaret, who thought that Sandy had rejected her when she didn't accept her first invitation. She wouldn't try inviting her a second time and risk another rejection.

Then we met Jeannie, who lacked the confidence to share with the women in her Bible-study group.

Third was Jim, a volcano about to erupt as he reluctantly took on every job that was pushed his way.

Let's look at these people one at a time and see what they can teach us about the principle of pretending confidence.

MARGARET. Full of hurt pride and fear that no one likes her, Margaret is realistic enough to know that if she doesn't try, she won't have any friends.

Margaret calls Sandy again, acting confident, even though she is scared to the core. Sandy sees a friendly woman who cares enough to try again.

The most important thing to remember in practicing what you don't feel is that, while it is acting, it is *not* acting like someone you're not. You'll only get into trouble if you try to pretend you're someone other than yourself. You are simply pretending you're not scared to death. For Margaret, it means making a phone call even when all her self-protective voices tell her not to risk it.

The Result. This time Sandy is free and says, "Oh, I'd love to go shopping with you. I've been so lonely trying to adjust to a new community." The women have a pleasant morning browsing through the local mall.

Margaret is amazed and elated. Whether she realizes it or not, something has started to change inside of her, if she can only keep up the momentum. By receiving that one little positive response, a small seed of confidence has been planted. This is a small triumph, but it has shown Margaret that she can do it if she doesn't give up. Each time she puts herself forward, and practices acting positive even though she feels hesitant, her confidence grows a little stronger.

JEANNIE. The women are discussing the subject of sin. Jeannie is feeling uncomfortable with the direction the discussion is taking, because it's sounding more and more like the consensus is to whitewash the issue. She knows that sin includes a lot more than murder or adultery.

Finally, with a quiet, hesitant voice, she says, "You know, I read a book last week on this subject, and one thing it said was . . ."

The Result. As Jeannie speaks, she looks around the room at the women. To her great surprise, she sees that some of them are nodding in agreement. One of the women says, "Jeannie's right. Something I read the other day said . . ." Suddenly the discussion gets a little deeper and a lot more meaningful.

Going home with a good feeling about herself, Jeannie realizes that she can speak up. It isn't so terrible. Each time she does and gets a positive response, she becomes a little more sure of herself and a little more confident in expressing her feelings and opinions. She begins to notice that some of the things she has to say are actually helpful to others in the group.

This gradual increase of confidence does not mean that Jeannie will become a talkative member of the group. That might not be consistent with Jeannie's personality even if she did become more confident. What is important in practicing positive behavior is not so much changing behavior but changing attitude. It is more important for Jeannie to understand that she does have something to share, that others are helped by her sharing, and that people aren't going to shake their heads in disgust because she sounds so stupid. Then when she does have something to contribute, she won't be so afraid to speak out.

JIM. "I can't believe it," he grumbles to his wife, hanging up the telephone in disgust. "Now they've asked me to be coordinator for the Vacation Bible School this summer."

"What did you say?" Seeing he is tense and angry, she hopes that he won't explode at her.

"I said I'd think about it. But I don't want to do it. I'm not good with groups of kids."

"Then tell them No," she says firmly.

"But who else will do it?" Jim feels trapped, but his wife's support has given him hope that there must be a way out.

"Jim, if you're going to hate doing it, what good will you be anyway? Just tell them No. They'll find someone else."

They talk about it for a while, and finally Jim makes the phone call. With a queasy stomach, for the first time, Jim says: "No, I'm sorry. It's just not something I feel I can do."

The Result. The initial result, of course, is that Jim's anger and tension vanish and are replaced by relief that he is not facing a task he absolutely dreads doing.

The next result comes when Jim hears the person on the other end of the phone say: "I can understand that, Jim. Thanks for being honest with me. We do have a couple of other names in mind that we can try."

All of a sudden Jim discovers that at least one person still likes and respects him if he says No. It took him forty-five years to finally say it, but just that once is enough to start the ball rolling. Jim can now learn to be selective, taking on the jobs he likes or feels he can do well and leaving the rest for others to do.

As Jim becomes more selective in the jobs he takes on, he finds the hostility disappearing, and his family finds him a nicer man to live with.

Once you have the not-good-enoughs, they don't just disappear overnight. They will probably never disappear completely. No matter how confident you might be feeling, that little voice always comes back to tell you that you are inadequate, you will fail, you will fall on your face, and others will not like you. Ignoring the voice and acting positive is a way of proving that the voice isn't true.

It's not easy to risk lowering the protective barriers we've built against hurt and rejection. Start small. Once you see that it works, once you see that others don't begin to ostracize you for being more assertive and confident, it gets easier.

But where do you start? Think about the way you walk into a room. Do you square your shoulders, hold your head high, and move into a group with an air of control and confidence? Or do you slouch in through the back door and find a corner to hide in? I was in the latter category for a long time. Give me a back row and as much anonymity as possible, thank you.

Pretending confidence simply gave me the chance to slowly build my confidence, from easy situations into the more difficult ones. Actually, entering a room is easy. You pretend you have it all together, and, amazingly, people treat you as though you do. Only the most outgoing people will make the trip back into a corner to try and draw out someone who has slunk in unnoticed, but everyone responds easily to someone who moves with confidence. As I began to accumulate small victories, each one slowly but surely instilled more confidence until I was feeling what I was acting.

Next, I began to take the initiative in relating to other people. Think about the things others do that make you feel good and accepted—and then do it for someone else. Instead of always holding back shyly, I started complimenting people when I found something about them I liked, be it their clothes or the way they sang that morning in church. Find something in people that you genuinely appreciate— and tell them so. It's an easy place to start because you know people won't reject you if you're telling them something nice about themselves!

After building my confidence to initiate conversations in that way, I started introducing myself to women I wanted to know or really working up my courage and inviting people to do things with me. It was very, *very* hard at first and still does not come easily for me. But I discovered that with each situation I mastered with feigned confidence, a small measure of genuine confidence was left in its place. Pretended confidence becomes real confidence when practiced long enough.

When I first felt the urge to become a speaker for the Christian Women's Clubs of Stonecroft Ministries, I could hear that little voice loud and clear: "It would be nice, sure, but you could never do it. What do you know about public speaking? You'll bore them stiff or come off looking like some sort of idiot. Don't try it; you'll only be sorry."

I was sure the urging was coming from God, but that little voice intimidated me. Because I didn't want to ignore a nudge from God, I decided to pursue the matter, but I did it less than wholeheartedly. First, I made tentative inquiries about the requirements. That's always a good start for someone with the not-good-enoughs because you can then take the list of requirements home and think about them for a while. And thinking means you aren't doing, and that means you aren't risking.

Much to my surprise, however, the woman I asked responded with an enthusiastic, "Are you thinking about becoming a speaker? That would be wonderful!" Positive responses like that always surprise someone with the not-good-enoughs. I actually began to feel a glimmer of hope that public speaking was a job in which I might not fail.

After hearing how to start the process of qualifying as a speaker, I thanked the woman and went home full of confidence. Whereupon I promptly let the whole matter drop for a while.

Then another woman gave me a little nudge, and I took another step. This time I made a tape of my testimony and gave it to a friend for feedback. She gave me some pointers on things I could do to improve it. She also gave me the address of an area representative to whom I needed to send a copy for official evaluation. I thanked her and let it drop again.

Until I got another nudge. Each nudge became positive verification for me that people thought I could do public speaking, that people actually wanted me to do it. And in the end, I had the confidence to follow through.

Every time I walk into a roomful of people waiting to hear me speak, I freeze up inside. The meal is placed in front of me, and I just stare at it, wondering how I'll ever choke any of it down. But then I start speaking, and God takes over. I am so sure I am doing what He wants me to do that I keep stepping out. And each time I speak and a woman comes up to me afterward and tells me how I touched her, the pretended confidence that I started out with becomes more and more genuine.

Because of my insecurities, I had planned to be a homemaker all my life, hidden safely behind my family. Let me stress that I am not putting down homemaking; I consider it to be the highest calling a woman with a family has. My plan, though, was to be a homemaker to the exclusion of all else because it was safe.

Now, besides the public speaking, I have also become a freelance writer. Writing is a killer profession for someone with the not-good-enoughs because rejection is written into the job description. Especially when you're just getting started, sometimes 98 percent of what you write is rejected. There would be days when that voice would start moaning: "Why have you gotten yourself into this now? Why on earth would you think that anyone is interested in anything you have to say? You're not a professional writer. Why, I bet the editors are sitting around having a good laugh over the stuff you send in."

It might seem easy to be a writer. After all, you don't have to see the editor's face. You get the same form rejection letter that everyone else gets, so you don't know whether you're being rejected merely because the publisher can't use the piece or whether you are a lousy writer. With no personal contact, it should be simple.

But it isn't. Rejection hurts, no matter how you receive it. I just had to keep plugging away, sending the manuscripts away, even when I felt like a loser. Soon I made a couple of small sales, and then one day a magazine wrote to ask if $175 was adequate payment for an article I had written. I laughed out loud. I would have paid them to publish it, and they were asking if $175 was enough? I took the check and cashed it right away, sure that they would realize their mistake any minute and ask for it back.

Each sale, even the smallest ones, gave me a bit more confidence that perhaps I could write. Perhaps I was on the right track. I felt in my heart that I could make a difference for people by sharing some of the things God had helped me through, and I believed that this was something He wanted me to do.

I started writing on a subject close to my heart that I really thought God wanted me to share. I wrote to encourage women who have negative emotions about mothering and also to suggest practical ways to overcome the emotions. The articles kept returning with rejection notices. "God, if You want me to write about this," I prayed in frustration, "why do the articles keep coming back?"

This was a pivotal point for me. I had the inner assurance that God had given me the desire to write on this topic to help other women. At the same time, I had the small voice saying: "You're mistaken. It's not God speaking to you; it's your own frantic desires. Of course the articles keep coming back; they're no good."

Which voice was I going to listen to? One day I was ready to quit; the next I was ranting and raving about the stupid editors who couldn't see what a great article they had. Finally a thought came to me. Maybe what I was writing about had too large a scope to be contained in short articles. Maybe it needed to be in a book.

A book? Me, write a book? You can imagine how the voice worked overtime on me then. But I took the small nugget of confidence that had accumulated from my other sales, and I went to work. I wrote night and day, not being able to stop once I had started. As soon as the manuscript was completed, I sent an outline and a couple of chapters to a publisher.

That day was agony for me. My mailman doesn't come until late afternoon, and it was all I could do not to grab that manuscript back out of the mailbox and hide it safely away where no one would ever, *ever* see it. I desperately feared the rejection of some unknown editor who would never even see me.

A publisher did buy the manuscript and did publish the book. And the pretended confidence it had taken to get the book manuscript into the mail and leave it there blossomed into something very real. Each step I took, each chance I took, brought me closer to believing in myself and feeling confident.

Practice confidence in spite of your feelings. It's not a magic formula. It's simply a way of building confidence, of helping you take control of your life instead of giving in to that nasty, negative little voice.

Chapter 8

Voices

If you see yourself as a failure, you will find some way to fail, no matter how hard you want to succeed. On the other hand, if you see yourself as adequate and capable, you will face life with more optimism and perform nearer your best.—Josh McDowell.

From now on, I will be more careful choosing topics to write about. During the process of writing about self-esteem, mine has sometimes felt severely trampled on. My solution was to say, "I can't write about this subject because I still haven't mastered it. I'm a failure. I will just put this manuscript away in the bottom of a drawer."

Does any of that sound familiar?

To my amazement, at one point in the writing process I realized God hadn't meant for me to write this book for you at all. He meant for me to write it for me because He still had so much to show me. I have been through some amazing self-discoveries during the past few months, and now, more than ever, I believe the truth in the words I've spoken here.

It was late at night, the time of day when I get most of my writing done. During the day, four children, one husband, five hundred loads of laundry, a kitchen full of dishes, a living room full of dust bunnies, and a TV running my favorite programs all conspire to keep me from writing. So it was late at night.

I sat at my computer, mostly just staring at the screen.

Once in a while my fingers would rat-a-tat on the keyboard; then I would shake my head and delete whatever I had written. The book just wasn't coming together, and I couldn't figure out why. When I had outlined it for the publisher, it had seemed so clear. Now I was stuck, wondering in what direction to go.

That's when I first heard the little voice. I've mentioned the little voice earlier in this book, so you understand by now I'm not talking about something audible. In fact, it might be better if you could actually hear it—then you could turn around and tell it to shut up! Instead, it creeps up slowly from your subconscious, and by the time you realize that it's talking, it's too late. You've already been listening so long it's nearly impossible to turn it off.

I really wasn't surprised to hear the voice, though I was disappointed. When you have the not-good-enoughs, you get used to the voice stalking you, waiting until you're feeling really up so it can start to tear you down.

You probably have heard the same kinds of things the voice said to me that night. "You mean you're still working on this piece of junk? Whatever for? You haven't listened to anything I've said, have you? Number one, you can't write. That first book was a fluke. Number two, even if you could write, you have nothing valuable to say. Who would want to plow through dozens of pages of your rubbish? And what about this subject matter? Why do you write about topics in which you're a failure? Self-esteem? Ha! You've never had any of that."

I tried to ignore the voice and keep on writing, but it wasn't long before I began buying into some of its message. In disgust I turned the computer off and went to bed, where I struggled to find the peace to sleep. The only thing that kept me from giving up that night was the certainty that morning's light would restore my perspective.

After all, I knew the information I was writing was accurate. I could follow my own suggestions and see that my self-doubts were unfounded. I decided to respond to each point.

Number one, I can write. I'm still learning, but I'm getting better. I don't think the publisher was asleep when it accepted my manuscript. Number two, I know I have something of value to say because I have received positive feedback on my first book.

The next point was subject matter. The voice was right; I still struggle against low self-esteem. Many people do. I never pretended that I had it all together. In fact, I tried to stress that I am still learning, still growing, in this area. So why am I so hard on myself, expecting perfection?

I answered the voice point by point and went to sleep. I woke up in the morning, surprised to find the voice still there. It followed me around all day, belittling everything I did. "I just need a break," I told myself. "I'll stop writing for a couple of days and distance myself from the subject matter."

A couple of days later, the voice was still following me around. I would come home from Bible study, and the voice would be saying, "Ran your mouth all day today, didn't you? Don't you think they might be getting a little tired of hearing your life story week after week?"

I would sit down to take a lunch break, and the voice would say, "Sitting down again? Look at this house! How can you sit there like some lazy so-and-so with all the work you should be doing?"

I would yell at the kids, and the voice would berate me. I would fight with my husband, and the voice would laugh at me. I would buy something at the store, and the voice would remind me that children were starving on the other side of the world.

I prayed repeatedly that God would remove the voice. I confessed everything I knew to confess; I worked hard at keeping a positive attitude even when I felt I was hanging on by my fingernails. Over and over again I reminded myself of the truth in hopes that it would drown out the voice. But it didn't.

Finally I put the manuscript in a drawer, hoping never to see it again. I kept telling myself I would start on it again the next day, when I had more time, or when the kids were in bed or when I didn't have a meeting to go to. But I knew I wasn't going to work on it—it was just getting too painful. Mentally, I began composing a letter to my editor, making excuses for a manuscript that would never be finished.

While part of me was listening to the voice and accepting failure, another part of me kept fighting. I finally realized that if God wasn't helping me out of this struggle, it was because I hadn't learned what He wanted me to learn yet.

It was hard to talk to people about what I was going through. Most would say something like, "Oh, Candy, why are you doing that to yourself? Why would you think such things about yourself?" It was my mother who first suggested that perhaps the voice was coming from Satan in an attempt to keep me from writing, to keep me from being effective, and to keep me from hearing the voice of God.

I had never considered that possibility before, but as soon as she said it, I knew it was true. So I did something startling. I accepted the voice as a fact of life. I told people that I had my own little hobgoblin perched on my shoulder, yakking away at me all day. I began to talk back to the voice, letting it know that I was refusing to believe it. When the voice persisted, I would pray, letting God fight the battle for me.

I came to the conclusion that it didn't matter whether I finished the book. God had indeed led me to write on the subject matter, but now I wasn't so sure whether it was because He wanted a published book out of it or whether it was His way of getting me to listen. I obviously still had a lot to learn about self-esteem.

I have already mentioned the first thing I learned from this experience. The little voice that puts you down doesn't always come from you. Sometimes it does, because bad habits are easily learned. But remember that the master of lies taught you the bad habit in the first place. The two things Satan works hardest at are keeping souls out of heaven and discouraging Christians, thus reducing their witness.

The second thing I learned is that a fine line divides pride and a healthy self-image. Inside of one person, self-loathing and self-aggrandizing can exist side by side. I realized how easy it would be for me to start patting myself on the back for my achievements—that perhaps I had even begun to do that very thing.

You see, I had thought that God was making my self-image strong and removing all the self-doubts. But what He really had done was take my weakness—a poor self-image—and bring glory to Himself through it or in spite of it.

In a letter, I was attempting to tell a friend about the voice and how desperately I was trying to pray it away. Groping for a way to make it clear, I said, "You know that place in the Bible where Paul says he had a thorn in the flesh, which he prayed for God to remove—but God chose not to remove it?"

Suddenly I felt a strong prompting to look up that scripture. I knew about the thorn in the flesh, and I knew that God wouldn't remove it, but I couldn't recall why God said He wouldn't remove it.

I found the passage in 2 Corinthians 12.

To keep me from becoming conceited because of these surpassingly great revelations, there was given me a thorn in my flesh, *a messenger of Satan, to torment me.* Three times I pleaded with the Lord to take it away from me. But he said to me, "My grace is sufficient for you, for my power is made perfect in weakness." Therefore I will boast all the more gladly about my weaknesses, so that Christ's power may rest on me. That is why, for Christ's sake, I delight in weaknesses, in insults, in hardships, in persecutions, in difficulties. For *when I am weak, then I am strong* (verses 7-10, NIV, emphasis supplied).

It is so hard to know where the fine line is drawn. A healthy self-image is absolutely necessary to function effectively, but just over the line is the pride that makes us forget we need God to take us each step of the way. We can make ourselves too self-sufficient if we are not careful!

Finally the voice let up. My editor called to see how the manuscript was progressing, and I finally pulled it out of the drawer. Some of the points that had been giving me trouble fell into place, and I was able to write some more.

Then it happened again. I was stalled, not knowing what direction to take. So instead of writing, I started reading. I had purchased a couple books about self-image, and I hoped that they would inspire me to continue writing.

Instead, God led me down yet another road of self-discovery, this one even more painful than the previous.

I came upon a passage that accurately described me and the way I handle personal relationships. I froze as I read it because the explanation given was identical to an event that had occurred in my own life as a child. I had never dealt with an instance of perceived rejection in my childhood, because I had never realized it was there.

God used the passage in that book to help me realize that the child who had been hurt was still inside of me. He also helped me realize something else—the person who had hurt me was not the one I knew in the present, because I have a good relationship with that person now. I love that person and feel no rejection today. I had to face the person from the past, the distorted image that had existed in my immature childhood mind.

I cried deep sobs of pain and rejection. I felt anger toward the person, knowing my anger was irrational but feeling it nevertheless. The next day I walked through my chores in a fog, still shaken to the core by my discovery. I spent the day asking God what I was supposed to do with this knowledge now that I had it. I considered confronting the person; I considered making an immediate appointment for counseling.

The next morning I knew the answer. When I awoke, the anger and hurt had subsided enough that I could listen to God. Without knowing how I knew, I knew the answer was simply this: I needed to forgive.

It was advice I had given others many times. Forgiving those who have wronged and hurt us is a necessary step in finding love for ourselves. I had not forgiven because I had not realized that much of the pain I suffered came from a hurting child huddling deep within me. Now I knew—now I could forgive.

I don't know whether that hurting child is gone; perhaps God has more to reveal. Maybe this is just a first step. But isn't that what developing self-worth is all about? Allowing God to help us take one step at a time, moving forward, picking ourselves up if we stumble, and watching God make it into something positive.

Recommended Reading

Alcorn, Randy, and Nanci Alcorn. *Women Under Stress: Preserving Your Sanity*. Portland, Ore.: Multnomah Press, 1986.
(Other books in this Touch of Grace Series from Multnomah Press include: *Becoming Complete: Embracing Your Biblical Image* by Marion Duckworth, and *Walking a Thin Line: Anorexia and Bulimia* by Pam Vredevelt and Joyce Whitman.)

Getz, Gene A. *Building Up One Another*. Wheaton, Ill.: Victor Books, 1983. (Other books by Gene A. Getz also published by Victor Books include: *Loving One Another*, *Encouraging One Another*, and *Praying For One Another*.)

LaHaye, Tim. *Increase Your Personality Power* (Pocket Guides Series). Wheaton, Ill.: Tyndale House Publishers, 1986.

_____. *Spirit Controlled Temperament: Strength for Every Weakness*. Wheaton, Ill.: Tyndale House Publishers, 1966.

Leman, Dr. Kevin. *The Birth Order Book*. Old Tappan, N.J.: Fleming H. Revell Co., 1985.

McDowell, Josh. *His Image . . . My Image*. San Bernardino, Calif.: Here's Life Publishers, Inc., 1985.

McMinn, Robert R. *Your Hidden Half: Blending Your Private and Public Self*. Grand Rapids, Mich.: Baker Book House, 1988.

Myers, T. Cecil. *You Can Be More Than You Are*. Waco, Tex.: Word Books, 1979.

Ward, Ruth M. *Self-Esteem: A Gift From God*. Grand Rapids, Mich.: Baker Book House, 1984.